"I am stunned by the terrible beauty of this story. As a grandmother and a mother, I feel the poignant emotions, and I'm so glad that the end of the story, which is yet to be revealed, involves joy and the wiping away of every tear."

— KAY WARREN,
author and speaker

"What an unspeakable gift. With compelling transparency and honesty Barbara and Rebecca invite us into the pain, sorrow, and joy of Molly's story. Your heart will be deeply moved as you absorb the impact of a little girl who lived here for only seven days and who is now whole and in God's presence. This book is a guide, a resource to help us navigate through the pain of loss. Reading *A Symphony in the Dark* is a tender, sacred experience."

— CRAWFORD AND KAREN LORITTS,
authors and speakers

"Can anything of lasting worth be achieved in a mere seven days? Molly's nine hidden months in the womb prepared her for a seven-day sprint of epic proportion. 'Every life *has* a divine purpose!' she shouted to us without uttering a word. After reading the opening paragraphs of *A Symphony in the Dark,* I remained riveted to the very end. And I left a tear on almost every page."

— TOM ELLIFF,
pastor, missionary, author

"Anyone who reads this book will be drawn into the story of a baby girl who was so treasured while she lived her few precious days on this earth. For the Raineys and Mutzes, and all who have said goodbye to a child on this side of Heaven, it is a high calling, a call to love sacrificially in the most literal way. That makes it a very difficult calling as well."

— MOLLY PIPER,
blogger at mollypiper.org, and mother of
Felicity Margaret, born into the arms of
the Savior.

"As we listen closely to the beautiful music played through the short life of little Molly Ann, what we will find between its sad rhyme and tragic meter are the very present triumphant notes being played by God's instruments of eternal life, healing, glory, joy, and redemption."

— KERRY HASENBALG,
Founding Director, Congressional
Coalition on Adoption Institute

A Symphony in the Dark

Hearing God's Voice *in* Seasons *of* Grief

BARBARA RAINEY *and*
REBECCA RAINEY MUTZ

a Symphony in the Dark

Hearing God's Voice *in* Seasons of Grief

BARBARA RAINEY *and*
REBECCA RAINEY MUTZ

FAMILYLIFE PUBLISHING®

A SYMPHONY IN THE DARK
Published by FamilyLife Publishing®
5800 Ranch Drive
Little Rock, Arkansas 72223
1-800-FL-TODAY · FamilyLife.com
A ministry of Campus Crusade for Christ International®

This book is not intended to replace the medical or psychological advice of a trained
medical professional. Readers are advised to consult a physician or other qualified
health-care professional regarding treatment of their medical problems. The authors and
publisher specifically disclaim liability, loss, or risk, personal or otherwise, which is
incurred as a consequence, directly or indirectly, of the use or application of any of the
contents of this book.

Unless otherwise indicated, all Scripture quotations are from The Holy Bible, English
Standard Version®, copyright © 2001 by Crossway Bibles, a publishing ministry of Good
News Publishers. Used by permission. All rights reserved.

Scripture quotations marked (NASB) are taken from the New American Standard Bible®,
Copyright © 1960, 1962, 1963, 1968, 1971, 1972, 1973, 1975, 1977, 1995 by The
Lockman Foundation. Used by permission. (www.Lockman.org)

Scripture quotations marked (NIV) are taken from the HOLY BIBLE, NEW INTERNA-
TIONAL VERSION®. NIV®. Copyright© 1973, 1978, 1984 by International Bible Society.
Used by permission of Zondervan. All rights reserved.

ISBN: 978-1-60200-304-0

Copyright © 2009 by Barbara Rainey and Rebecca Rainey Mutz

All rights reserved. No part of this book may be reproduced or transmitted in any form or
by any means, electronic or mechanical, including photocopy, recording, or any
information storage and retrieval system, without permission in writing from the publisher.
Requests for permission to make copies of any part of this publication should be sent to:
permissions@FamilyLife.com

FamilyLife Publishing® is a registered trademark of FamilyLife®

Design: Brand Navigation

Photographs on cover, and pages 34, 64, 84, 98, and 146 from HL Concepts

Image on page 82 from StockByte

Printed in the United States of America

2009—First Edition

12 11 10 09 1 2 3 4 5

DEDICATION

To the millions of babies and children around the world

who are living and dying alone

who do not know the deep love of family

whose only value is in their growing statistics.

May Molly's life inspire an army of lovers

who will go near to sacrifice for the least of these.

CONTENTS

When I hear Handel, Beethoven, or Bach, I think how profoundly moving music can be. I feel my soul lifted, called to something higher, something nobler, something more perfect than this fallen world has to offer. It invades my mundane, ordinary existence and as I listen I feel transported—as if the music has escaped from another realm.

A grand and glorious symphony has been written, and for seven dark but beautiful days I heard the strains of its melody. The musical score came from Heaven with the debut of a tiny, helpless baby. Her song was complex, yet perfectly written.

Frail as she was, this little one took center stage and, without uttering a sound, stirred the passions of the thousands who listened.

Elegant music has a lingering effect. And so did the hymn of this tiny life. She touched me and I am left with the divinely beautiful memory, changed forever by having heard a few measures of His symphony in her brief but mighty life.

Be still and listen. May you, too, feel the wonder of this great mystery, that one so small could lead so many to hear the Everlasting Song.

Barbara Rainey

Waiting on

Waiting on Baby

I will give you the treasures of darkness

And hidden wealth of secret places,

So that you may know that it is I,

The Lord, the God of Israel,

who calls you by your name.

— ISAIAH 45:3 (NASB)

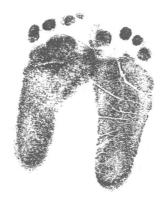

Today marks forty weeks plus seven days for my daughter in her first pregnancy. First babies are often late, but that is of little comfort to her. She tries to fill her overdue days with getting her nails done, baking, going with a friend to the pool—anything to not think about how long this child is taking to make its entrance into the world.

The rest of the family has been waiting too. Not like Rebecca, of course, but I've not planned anything for the last week because I'd planned to be with her. I've changed my plane tickets twice already. If she doesn't deliver tomorrow, I'll have to change them again!

For days I've been packed for travel, and Rebecca has been packed for the hospital. Everyone in the family jumps when a phone rings and the caller ID shows either Rebecca's or Jacob's name.

As we've talked about waiting on the baby, I've been reminded about how we have to wait on so many things in life: waiting in the checkout line at the store, waiting in traffic during rush hour, waiting for school to start, waiting for school to end, waiting for summer, waiting for graduation, waiting to get married, waiting for a job, waiting to get pregnant. We wait on God's timing in these and so many other situations in life.

While we wait, God is at work. He is still at work with Rebecca and Jacob's new little life, this baby who still has a few more hours—hopefully, just a few—of being knit together in its mother's womb.

God is at work in the hidden places.

He is at work in the waiting.

And as we wait our choice is to trust Him and His timing, to rest in the knowledge that He does all things well.

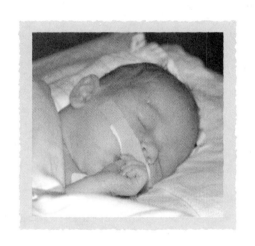

A New

Kind of

A New Kind of Waiting

How God governs all events in the universe without sinning and without removing responsibility from man, and with compassionate outcomes is mysterious! But it's what the Bible teaches. God "works all things after the counsel of His will" (Ephesians 1:11).

— JOHN PIPER

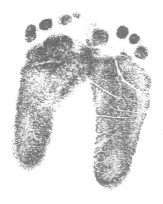

Great news: Jacob and Rebecca's baby has been born—a girl! We rejoice at the arrival of little Miss Molly Ann!

Bad news: Something is wrong.

My husband, Dennis, and I have been tracking with Jacob and Rebecca since last evening when her contractions started, and they left for the hospital around 7:00. We went to bed expecting to be awakened by a phone call, but we didn't hear anything in the night. Dennis woke up at 4:00 and sent a text message to Jacob:

"What's up?"

Jacob texted back, "She's beginning to push."

Then we got another text at 5:45 a.m. saying, "It's a girl!"

Then nothing for ninety minutes.

We learn later that Molly didn't cry for four minutes, and doctors suspected she had a heart murmur. She has been taken to the neonatal intensive care unit (NICU) at Children's Hospital. It's good that we have such units, but it's bad when your baby has to go there.

So now a new kind of waiting has begun. It's four in the afternoon on Friday, and I'm on a plane from Little Rock, Arkansas, bound for Denver, Colorado. I can't get there fast enough. Dennis has left on a different flight. We both changed our travel plans so many times that we'll arrive separately at the airport and meet to go to the hospital together. We don't know much more than we did shortly after Molly's birth. Doctors have come and gone and the new parents, who got no sleep last night because of labor, now can't sleep for concern over their precious baby. They are waiting for any signs of hope in tone of voice or words coming from the medical team.

Sorting through all of this, I think of Psalm 27:14: "Wait for the LORD; be strong, and let your heart take courage; wait for the LORD!" It is good to know that God knows. He has all the answers, knows all the plans, all the purposes and above all He always intends good for His children. That is our comfort as we wait. As one of my favorite writers, Andrée Seu has said, "It is a good thing to wait upon Him in a well-watered land. It is a [holy] thing to wait upon Him in a barren landscape."[1]

It seems we are entering a holy waiting place.

When we arrive at Children's Hospital, we are met in the waiting room by our son-in-law, Jacob. He is somber and delivers the news that it is not Molly's heart that is the problem; something is wrong in her brain. We are stunned.

Dennis would tell me later that his first thoughts were: *You can work on a heart. It's still dangerous, but it can be repaired. But brain surgery? That's altogether more serious.*

Jacob then takes us, along with our son Ben, who'd picked us up at the airport, to see Molly. The movement of her little chest makes it clear that her heart is laboring. Jacob tells us that her oxygen level is very low, only 45. It should be 95 to 100. I slip off to the lactation room where Rebecca is learning to pump breast milk. I drop to my knees in front of her and she collapses on my shoulder, sobbing. I have nothing to say. We just cry together.

The landscape is barren. It does not feel holy.

But God is near.

When Facing the Unknown

Worry looks at God through the circumstances.
Peace looks at the circumstances through God.[2]
— ADRIAN ROGERS

There is a rhythm to life, certainties that we count on. We know that the sun will rise each new day and that the seasons will continue to follow one after the other. The Bible tells us in Genesis 8:22: "While the earth remains, seedtime and harvest, cold and heat, summer and winter, day and night, shall not cease."

Yet even when our daily lives become boringly predictable, the truth is we do not know what tomorrow will bring. From our human perspective, the future is a vast unknown.

When Rebecca and Jacob welcomed little Molly Ann into the world, it was with the expectation and hope that she would be healthy and whole. While it is a wondrous miracle that tiny babies are born perfectly formed day after day, year after year, generation after generation, there is no guarantee. And so our families face the apprehension of unanswered questions: What is the extent of her medical problems? Can they be fixed? How long will this last? When can she go home? The joy of this new, beautiful life is smothered by a cloud of anxiety.

One of my heroines of the faith, Corrie ten Boom, a holocaust survivor of the Ravensbrook Concentration Camp, said, "Worry does not empty tomorrow of sorrow; it empties today of strength."[3] This present unknown threatens to drain us of strength. Yet, while we feel like deflated beach balls, born to fly in the summer sun but sucked of air and life, we still hope for a solution to breathe life back into our souls.

As we wait, we remind ourselves that there is more—much more—of which we can be certain.

God is the Creator and Sustainer of life—"For you created all things, and by your will they existed and were created" (Revelation 4:11).

He is the Lord of our days—"In your book were written, every one of them, the days that were formed for me, when as yet there was none of them" (Psalm 139:16).

He is good in all that He does—"No one is good except God alone" (Luke 18:19). Only God can act in pure goodness, untarnished by selfish or evil motives.

So as Rebecca and Jacob and both extended families wait to understand what God already knows and has purposed for little Molly, we do so, believing in His great goodness and loving control over the affairs of our lives. As the psalmist wrote in Psalm 56:3–4:

When I am afraid, I put my trust in you. In God, whose word I praise, in God I trust; I shall not be afraid.

"Life wouldn't be so hard if we didn't expect it to be so easy."[4]

—MICK YODER,
father of Benji who died at six years of age in a small-plane crash

Joy Turned to Fear

As soon as Molly was born and the doctor proclaimed that she was a girl, I was so relieved, so excited. For some reason I had prepared for a boy because that was all I heard about when I was pregnant.

The doctor cut the cord, laid her on my tummy, and Molly and I locked eyes and hearts. She had dark, beautiful hair. How perfect she looked and how cool that God made her part of me and part of Jacob. I stroked her head with my left hand and wanted to pull her close to me. She wasn't making any noises, and the nurses on either side of me said she should be crying but wasn't. They took her from me to *a little table across the room and told me that they were going to check her out and get a good cry out of her.*

I was numb and tired, and had no idea that Molly not crying was a bad sign. So when the nurses took her, I was a little anxious but didn't know enough to be scared. I was just in awe that we had a little girl.

Three or four nurses worked on Molly, but I wasn't hearing anything. I kept asking, "Is something wrong? Is she okay?" Even though I started to worry a little, everything was dreamlike. They were all busy working on her. Jacob was going back and forth between Molly and me, taking video. Our friend Lara Veve was taking pictures and came over once to show me a shot of Molly with one eye open, which was sweet and made us laugh.

Then the nurses told us that they were going to take Molly to the NICU because they wanted to get her on oxygen. I couldn't go because they still had to fix me up, so Jacob went with Molly. Resigned to my bed, I decided to make the best of it. I got my computer and my phone so I could share our news and ask people to pray.

Jacob was following what was happening and let me know that the doctors thought Molly might have a heart murmur, though they weren't really sure so they were going to do some tests.

When I talked to my older sister Ashley and told her about the heart murmur, fear must have come through my voice. She reassured me and said not to worry about what might happen—just enjoy Molly. That small bit of encouragement set the tone for the rest of the week. I made a choice in that moment to enjoy our daughter as long as we had her.

As the morning dragged on, it was really hard to have to stay where I was and not be with Molly. She was born at 5:27 a.m. and it was nearing 10:00 a.m., and this child I had carried for nine months was now in the care of others. When the nurses finally allowed me to be wheeled down to see Molly, I was taken by the beauty of our daughter and sad at the same time. Molly was attached to all these wires, a little cuff on her hand to measure her oxygen intake, a warmer on her foot, a round plastic hood over her head to deliver oxygen. The doctors told us they were going to take Molly to Children's Hospital for more tests. But before they did, both Mommy and Daddy got a chance to hold our little girl. It was a sweet moment for us, holding our daughter close to our hearts before we watched her be loaded into a protective cube that would take her to Children's.

After Molly left, Jacob got in bed with me as gingerly as possible, and held me while I cried. I was in pain but my heart hurt more than my body did. We soon both fell asleep from exhaustion.

When we woke up we wanted to get back into task mode for Molly. So we went home to get clothes and necessary items for bringing her home, and headed to Children's Hospital.

When I saw her, I just lost it, sobbing. She looked so different, sprawled on her back with no blankets, coverings, or socks. Just one little diaper. She had a tube down her throat for oxygen, an IV in her head, another tube in her belly-button for food, and an assortment of wires and stickers plastered everywhere over her little body. She had the hiccups, which in utero had always made me laugh. Now, shaking her tiny body covered in tubes, they seemed scary.

Jacob was asking the doctor all kinds of questions, but I chose to ignore it all and just focus on Molly. I didn't care about the medical jargon floating around, just that our sweet baby needed me and I needed her. I became numb to all the machines, the beeping, the numbers, the wires. It was overwhelming.

My parents arrived an hour or two later and we all embraced and cried again. Jacob and I introduced them to Molly and examined her long feet and soft hair. My dad joined Jacob in asking questions of the doctors and nurses. My mom and I oohed and ahhed over our little girl.

By then it was nearing 11:00 p.m., and we decided to go back to our house and sleep in our own bed rather than in a fold-out couch a floor away from Molly. We would return as soon as possible the following morning. But leaving Molly that night was so hard. I felt so empty and still so very tired.

A Severe Testing

The suffering caused by shattered dreams must not be thought of

as something to relieve if we can or endure if we must.

It's an opportunity to be embraced, a chance to discover our desire

for the highest blessing God wants to give us, an encounter with Himself!

— LARRY CRABB

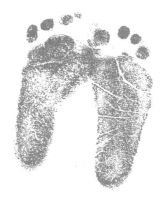

After a fitful night, the four of us—Jacob, Rebecca, Dennis, and I—return to the hospital. At 11:00 a.m. we are walking behind tiny little Molly as she is wheeled down several long hallways to undergo a series of medical tests—x-rays, an ultrasound, and an MRI. The new parents are forced to again release their infant to the care of technicians who are holding her lines, tubes, and fragile body. *Will Molly feel any pain? Will she be cold? Will they be gentle with her?* My heart longs for her to be comforted by her mother, scooped up and cradled in her arms.

But now is not the time.

A radiologist makes a copy of several pages from a textbook that describes the suspected malformation in Molly's brain. While Dennis and Jacob wait for these to print, Rebecca and I reluctantly go back upstairs to Molly's empty room.

When Dennis comes back to the room, he sets up his laptop to do some further research online. I am grateful that he is doing this. Like Rebecca, I don't want to be bothered by scary facts; I only want to enjoy Molly and remain hopeful. (A friend of ours later said, "Maternal denial runs deep.") Husbands and fathers are created by God to be providers and protectors, wired to find solutions for those in their care. Our two men, new father Jacob and Molly's Papa have begun that search for information and potential solutions.

With their quick research, it doesn't take long to find out that Molly has a serious abnormality in the middle of her brain—something very rare and very destructive. It's not the kind of information one ever wants to discover. A heart murmur sounds so simple now. How we wish that were all we were dealing with.

Around 3:00 p.m., we are sitting in a private windowless room with a neurologist, a cardiologist, a neonatologist, and Molly's nurse. They are giving us the news that more than 50 percent of Molly's brain is already damaged on both sides. She is blind and will likely never speak. With multiple delicate and risky surgeries, she might be able to have some functions, but they can't really say for sure.

Devastated is not a strong enough word to describe how we feel.

We are heartbroken. Stunned. In anguish. This feels like a free fall into a dark black hole. Our minds frantically grasp for anything solid as we ask, "What now?"

Later Dennis is able to connect with a friend who has been a neurologist for thirty years. He puts the situation in perspective: "In cases like Molly's, where there is so much brain damage, I've never seen a good outcome through surgery."

Never is a strong word.

News beyond comprehension.

Joy turned to mourning.

The facts are clear—it will take a miracle for Molly to live.

When the News Is Bad

God is behind everything, but everything hides God. [1]

We humans are afraid of pain. No one likes to hurt. We avoid it, mask it, and run from it, refusing to get close to pain even when it is not our own. We shy away from stories like Molly's because we are afraid that if we get too close God might infect us with the same kind of experience—as if it were a disease that could spread by contact. Fear can make us superstitious and irrational.

But God does not act haphazardly.

Good and beauty can be found in the experience of loss if we are willing to embrace it. But finding the good and beautiful is only possible when we believe that God is lovingly sovereign, that pain is not random, not without origin, not without purpose.

This truth is evident in the story of Job, who knew a level of pain and loss beyond what most humans will ever endure. None of what happened to him was by chance; it was God who suggested that the evil one, Satan, consider Job as the most honorable of men living on the earth at that time. And then, shockingly to our way of thinking, God permitted Satan to inflict pain on Job.

What kind of God is this?

The story flies in the face of all we want to be true. It doesn't make sense to us that someone who is living rightly should suffer so profoundly. It seems terribly contradictory. One should be rewarded for making good choices, right? Where is the fairness in God's actions? Why not let Satan loose on those who deserve it?

These are the things we consider as we begin to absorb the devastating news that Molly probably will not live. We remember what Job did and said when he received the staggering news that all ten of his children had been killed. Job tore his robe in anguish and fell to the ground devastated. But there, pressed into the dirt by an enormous burden of grief, he also worshipped God, saying, "Naked I came from my mother's womb, and naked shall I return.

The LORD gave, and the LORD has taken away; blessed be the name of the LORD" (Job 1:21). Job knew that he came into this world with nothing, that all he had was given to him by God, and he believed it was God's to take away.

We, the parents and grandparents of Molly, believe that too. God created her; she belongs to Him.

We also believe that death is in fact a disease that infects all of humanity, yet we know with certainty that God never intended that we should die. Death feels so wrong to all who face it because it is so wrong. Intuitively we feel the discord, the incongruity that screams, "This should not be!" that strongly suggests there is another way. This clash within is a call to our hearts to believe the gospel.

As an artist, I've learned to understand that the beauty in a truly great painting is most often seen in the expert use of light and dark. The focus of a painting, the most important element the artist wants the viewer to see, is made more dramatic by putting the lightest lights next to the darkest darks. In the same way, beautiful music is a masterful blend of deep reverberating notes rising purposefully to lilting sweet sounds. Symphonies tell stories of dark anguish and struggle while building to a crescendo of victory and triumph.

Likewise, the Creator of all beauty knows that in His living works of art and song the most beautiful are those who have known the darkness of pain and loss, thereby magnifying the lightness of great joys and delights. Truly the experience of death makes the experience of the gift of life all the more precious and beautiful. This, I believe, is the message of Romans 8:28: "And we know that for those who love God all things work together for good, for those who are called according to his purpose."

"How unfathomable the thought of losing a child was to me. You can imagine what it would be like to lose your child if you have had a child. What you cannot imagine is the grace I have physically had during this time. I can actually feel the Lord holding me as we go through this."

— ANONYMOUS MOTHER WHO TOOK HER TWELVE-
YEAR-OLD DAUGHTER OFF LIFE SUPPORT

It Was All About Molly

When Jacob and I arrived back at Molly's room, we had eyes only for her. But the sight of her was again alarming. She was still lying on her back, not moving, with all those tubes and wires attached to her. Beneath it all was her sweet little body, so perfectly formed. Only then we had no idea something inside wasn't so perfectly formed. We hugged her, kissed her, traced her skin with our fingers and lips, talked to her, and cried over her.

My parents joined us later and took pictures of us leaning over her bed as we whispered our love into her ear, asking her the questions only parents do: How *did you sleep last night? Are you cold? Do you know how much Mommy and Daddy love you?*

We made sure she had a blanket at all times, whether it was the green blanket made by her Aunt Ashley or the soft pink and floral one with ruffles, a gift from one of our friends. We wanted people to know our girl was all snuggly in her bed.

When Molly was brought back to her room after the MRI, her nurse asked us if we wanted to hold our little girl. I said yes, but wanted to make sure I wasn't going to hurt her in any way. Jacob looked at me when I asked if he would like to hold her and he said he wasn't sure.

"I am hesitant to get too emotionally connected," he explained.

In Jacob's mind, not holding Molly might make it easier should anything happen. I gently encouraged him to experience the joy of embracing his daughter. I told him that he was missing out on an incredible joy of bonding with his daughter and loving her in a unique way. After I held her for some time, I passed her off to Jacob and watched as he joyfully took her into his heart. It was clear to see that he loved being a daddy.

Later that afternoon, I was busy in the lactation room when Jacob came in and told me I needed to finish because some doctors wanted to talk to us about Molly's MRI results. I was annoyed to have to hurry with something that couldn't be rushed. He told me he thought they were going to give us bad news, saying, "It doesn't take that many doctors to give good news." I pushed his reasoning aside, thinking he was being too pessimistic.

When I came into the hallway, the medical team was there and they were smiling, but their smiles weren't "things are fine" expressions, more just a courtesy. They led us into a room that was marked PRIVATE FAMILY ROOM, and I thought, This can't be good.

The doctors explained the details of Molly's condition, that the MRI showed she had irreversible brain damage, more than 50 percent, and that it would affect her physical life functions. It could take ten to twenty serious surgeries to help Molly live, if she would even survive surgery.

We were stunned, shocked, numbed by their words. I kept thinking: But we're at Children's Hospital—they can fix this. I asked the doctor, "What would you do?"

He said, "Do you want the truth?"

I thought, Yes, otherwise I wouldn't have asked! But I said, "Of course."

"I would make her comfortable," he said. "I would just enjoy her while you have her."

We sat there, incapable of moving. Then we were weeping. Jacob and I grabbed each other and melted into each other's arms.

This was the worst news I'd ever heard in my life. I felt as though the world had ended. Hearing, "She needs brain surgery or heart surgery"—that's hard. But hearing, "There's really nothing we can do . . . " was a death sentence.

The doctors left and my parents stayed, crying with us and reading some Psalms.

I felt a huge desire to go back to Molly's room. I didn't want to spend my time with any more doctors or in any more meetings. Suddenly all I wanted was to be with Molly, to savor every moment with her.

That night we spent some time calling our siblings and Jacob's parents, crying and sharing the news and asking them to come meet our daughter. Speaking with Lori, Jacob's sister, was encouraging. As we wrestled with our choices, she said, "Letting your daughter be with Jesus would be the most unselfish thing to do."

Sometime after midnight, as I lay down to sleep my last thought was, "I just want to make time stand still."

Waiting fo

Waiting for Heaven

The moment you enter the Valley of the Shadow of Death,

things change. You discover that Christianity is not something doughy,

passive, pious, and soft . . . The life of belief teems with thrills,

boldness, danger, shocks, reversals, triumphs, and epiphanies.

— TONY SNOW

Heaven

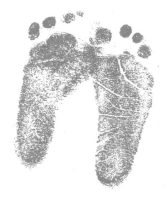

Dennis and I wake up to the memory that Molly's problems are irreversible. This is not just a bad dream. We spent most of yesterday in tears and we know the day ahead will be another difficult one. Family members are flying in to meet Molly and to grieve with Rebecca and Jacob.

How will we endure the days to come? It seems impossible to walk this road to death with one so tiny, so undeserving of such a quick end. It's clear Molly will not survive, and I begin to wonder, *Will we?*

Again we cling to all we know to be true. The certainty of Heaven is our rock. Knowing we will see Molly again makes the present agony bearable. Faith in the unchanging promise of God to never leave us or forsake us gives us strength.

Throughout the day, a steady stream of family arrives. Jacob's parents, Bill and Pam Mutz, come first. Rebecca and Jacob proudly introduce them to Molly. Grandpa Bill has his camera in action almost immediately. He is the curator of capturing family moments, and we love him for it!

From all corners of the country, many siblings and some of their spouses also come to join in loving on Molly and her parents: Cari and Phil, Lori and Seth, Kelli, Ben and Marsha Kay, Samuel and Stephanie, Ashley, and Laura. Rebecca and Jacob delight in introducing their first-born daughter, wanting everyone to see her and kiss on her and love her with them. Some kneel at Rebecca's feet and cry as she holds Molly on a pillow on her lap, tethered to the life support systems. As each one arrives the flood gates open, releasing one wave of emotion after another. It is exhausting but it is right—and healthy—to mourn with those who mourn.

Even though we are awash in tears of grief, this day is beautiful as we begin hearing echoes of a love song. Sounds of music in the depth of love that embrace Molly's parents. Heavenly notes of glory in Molly's precious life.

Waiting for Heaven is not just what we are doing today, but what we do every day. I get so busy with the details of living that the focus on my destination is blurred. But now that Molly has come, Heaven is more clearly in sight. That which really matters is staring us in the face.

Heaven is knocking now, calling Molly home.

When All Hope Is Gone

One of the brightest, bonniest babies ever seen, he was the delight and expectation of our hearts; but the gift was claimed suddenly, and the child, who was to have done, according to our ideas, so much service on earth, went to sing God's praises with the angels! [1]

— MRS. C. H. SPURGEON

Rebecca has said over and over, "I just can't believe this is happening." She is stunned by this awful reality and is feeling not just the imminent loss of Molly, but the loss of all the dreams she had for a lifetime of living with her daughter. It just feels so wrong to her. Death is unnatural.

And yet, at the same time, the hope of Heaven feels so right. The longing Jacob and Rebecca already feel—knowing they will see their daughter again—is real. To lose a child with no hope of seeing her again, no hope of knowing her or being with her again someday would lead only to despair.

We are born with a deep desire to know perfect love. Our souls thirst for it. In the beginning, it was our destiny. Families were meant to mirror what God created us to experience with Him—a relationship completely free of discord.

In his book *Heaven*, Randy Alcorn writes:

We are homesick for Eden. We're nostalgic for what was implanted in our hearts. It's built into us, perhaps even at a genetic level. We long for what the first man and woman once enjoyed—a perfect and beautiful Earth with free and untainted relationships with God, each other, animals, and our environment. Every attempt at human progress has been an attempt to overcome what was lost in the Fall. [2]

As our family gathers to support, love, and encourage Jacob and Rebecca, we are talking freely about Heaven. We talk about how Molly might arrive in Heaven, riding on the back of Aslan [3] or carried by mighty angels. We talk about what Molly might see and do. We talk about her dancing with Jesus and laughing with joy in His presence. We take comfort in knowing she will never experience the pains and losses of life on earth.

The sounds of hope are becoming clearer, easier to hear.

We are grieving the certain loss of Molly while having the certain hope of seeing her again. It is a very different experience to grieve with hope than to grieve without it. Our confidence in the reality of Heaven is rooted in the many verses in the Bible that speak of its existence as a real place inhabited by real people, including Jesus Himself:

But we do not want you to be uninformed, brothers, about those who are asleep [those who have died], that you may not grieve as others do who have no hope. For since we believe that Jesus died and rose again, even so, through Jesus, God will bring with him those who have fallen asleep. (1 THESSALONIANS 4:13–14)

And I heard a loud voice from the throne saying, "Behold, the dwelling place of God is with man. He will dwell with them, and they will be his people, and God himself will be with them as their God. He will wipe away every tear from their eyes, and death shall be no more, neither shall there be mourning nor crying nor pain anymore, for the former things have passed away. And he who was seated on the throne said, "Behold, I am making all things new." (REVELATION 21:3–5A)

Heaven is far more real than what we know on earth. The knowledge that there will be no more pain or tears or mourning gives us strength to go forward in expectation. To know a place where all things will be new brings the distant song nearer to our hearts.

Death is inevitable; no one escapes it. Because this is true, it's imperative that we make Heaven our destination when our turn comes to depart this earth. Heaven is not a fairytale. It can be our home. As C. H. Spurgeon said, "To come to Thee is to come home from exile, to come to land out of the raging storm, to come to rest after long labor, to come to the goal of my desires and the summit of my wishes." [4]

"God knows what it is like to have to sit by

and watch a beloved only child die."

—MORNA COMEAU,
mother of two infant boys who died at birth
from Potter's syndrome

Introducing Our Sweet Pea

Jacob and I got up from a rough night of crying, talking, asking questions, and very little sleep. We were now staying in the hospital, just down the hall from Molly's room. I began a habit of going to her room when I woke up early each morning. I would sit quietly by her bed, tell her good morning, ask her questions, reflect on the past day's events and tell her about who had been to see her and how much we loved her.

I'd kiss her and she would open her eyes and she would look at me. At least I thought she was looking at me. The doctor said she was probably blind, but I ignored that.

She appeared so perfect. She didn't look like anything was wrong with her. The only thing that I could see that looked different was her heart pounding away in her little chest. Both Jacob and I admitted that on several occasions we felt as if we could take her away from all the tubes and wires and that she'd be okay.

Sometimes after being with her for a little bit, to ensure she was still with us, I would go back to our room and get back in bed for another hour or so of sleep. Then Jacob and I would get up for the day and get moving. Neither of us cared about showering, and I didn't put on the slightest bit of makeup the entire week. We just dressed and headed straight for her room, me with my hospital water jug and Jacob with our cell phones and morning coffee.

On Molly's third day of life, we ushered in many of her aunts and uncles and Jacob's parents and grandparents, Bob and Karen Gaiser, to meet her and gaze on her sweet face. Everyone cried and smiled and commented about how beautiful she was. When Cari and Phil, Jacob's sister and brother-in-law, arrived, the four of us hugged each other tightly and with such a connection. Having lost their infant daughter, Gracie, we could see how broken they were for us and that they knew how our hearts felt. The same was true with Jacob's parents, who lost their second born, Jonathan. They held us tightly, comforting us in a way that spoke volumes of their pain and ours.

We snapped more pictures with grandparents, aunts, and uncles standing over Molly as Jacob or I held her in the big yellow and green chair. I wanted to make sure we had a remembrance of all who came to see her and what their visit was like. There was so much I wanted to do in our short time, so much to share. I didn't want anyone to miss out on meeting our daughter. If I were to show you pictures, you would see sorrow and tears, and you would see joy and light.

Sometime that day, in between visitors, I was holding Molly. I was exhausted and decided I wanted to take a little nap with her, something I might not get to do any other time. I leaned back in the recliner, careful to keep Molly's tubes and wires from being stretched, and suddenly all was quiet. People left us alone to have uninterrupted quiet time together. Molly was back with me, I thought, where she's safe and nothing can hurt her.

When I awoke, my sisters, Laura and Ashley, had just arrived. Laura came with a pair of pink earrings for me that she felt honored Molly in all her "girly-ness." Ashley came in the room crying, hugged me, knelt next to my chair, and took in Molly's beauty. She gazed at her hair, her long feet, her delicate fingers. She lovingly caressed her sweet skin. Ashley later encouraged me to read a story to Molly and share some of the journal I had written to her before she was born.

Later that day, as Jacob was holding Molly he decided to read her one of his favorite books from childhood, The Mysterious Tadpole. *He read it with different voices and would look down at her in between paragraphs. Reading to her created sweet moments for both of us, memories we will always cherish.*

Before the day was done, Jacob and I spent more time talking about our choices regarding Molly's life and the various surgeries she could undergo. We continued to pray and ask God for direction and healing for our daughter.

Jacob was wrestling.

I simply wanted God to heal Molly, yet somehow I felt she was going to be with Jesus soon.

Enjoying th

Enjoying the Moments

Through trials, God bids us to choose: Do we believe, or do we not?
Will we be bold enough to love, daring enough to serve, humble
enough to submit, and strong enough to acknowledge our limitations?
Can we surrender our concern in things that don't matter so that we
might devote our remaining days to things that do?

— TONY SNOW

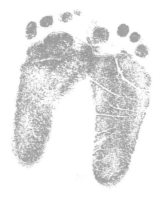

Rebecca and Jacob are the very proud parents of four-day-old Molly Ann, but the joy of being new parents is strangely mixed with the sorrow of her impending death.

Another difficult meeting was scheduled for today, this one including a leading interventional radiologist who offers to try the high-risk brain surgery. But the facts leave us staggering again as Rebecca and Jacob, along with Bill and Pam and Dennis and I, ask the doctors more questions. In the end the answers do not change; surgery would be life-threatening with no guarantees. Medically, there's not a glimmer of hope.

Our sweet daughter-in-law has been praying for Jesus to come back before Molly dies so Rebecca and Jacob can be spared this sorrow. We know that is not likely to happen. There's really no escaping. Waiting is our only option.

Waiting, and enjoying the moments.

It's been interesting to see how focused Rebecca and Jacob have become on maximizing every moment—capturing every detail, taking hundreds of photos and hours of video, reading stories to Molly, saying prayers over her. God is giving all of us an opportunity to encounter a holy pulling away from our normal, hectic lives. He's giving us an experience of His presence when all the trappings of life have become suddenly so very unimportant. The glitter is gone.

Rebecca has asked all family members who come to the hospital to write baby Molly a letter in her journal. Our son and daughter-in-law ask if they may read their entries to Molly. It's a powerful moment as he speaks to her of Heaven and his hope of running with her someday. (Samuel has a neuromuscular disease.) It will be an uncontainable joy for all of us who love these two, Samuel and Molly, who are handicapped on earth, to see their bodies whole one day in Heaven. Molly's approaching death invites us to hope, to look forward—way beyond earthly life and limitations. Ultimately, she invites us to see redemption, to see glory.

This little princess of the King helps us to hear His music.

The highlight of the day is Molly's dedication service. Grandpa Mutz and Papa Rainey lead the family, all fourteen of us crowded into Molly's small room, in reading scriptures, offering prayers of thanksgiving, and dedicating Molly's life to God. We weep, knowing we are dedicating Molly to God's service not on earth, but in Heaven. And then, with several of us kneeling at Rebecca's feet as she holds her sweet Molly, we sing:

> Turn your eyes upon Jesus,
> Look full in His wonderful face,
> And the things of earth will grow strangely dim
> In the light of His glory and grace.[1]

This present darkness is turned into a declaration of victory by faith. The easier thing would be to resign, to passively accept defeat. But by banding together and expressing faith in the midst of crisis we declare to those who could hear, including the multi-tudes of unseen ones, that we will still believe.

As the service ends, Rebecca and Jacob's siblings begin to leave for flights back to jobs and families. The four grandparents spend much of the evening sitting in silence, listening to our two young adults talk about heavy issues: getting second and third opinions, removing life support, funeral arrangements. They agonize over each topic, going back and forth between resting in what appears to be God's will and questioning what their responsibility for Molly's well-being is.

"If love could heal," Dennis said, "Molly would be whole and well."

God is good. I believe that with all my heart, but it's impossible not to feel that this shouldn't be happening.

When a Family Is Strongest

A family is meant to be the environment where human beings
can find shelter, warmth, protection and safety in each other.
It is to be a shelter in the time of storm. [2]

— EDITH SCHAEFFER

When Rebecca told me of Jacob's initial hesitation to hold Molly for fear of getting too attached, I thought how wise it was of her to encourage him to engage. That was all he needed anyway, one gentle nudge. After that, he was all in.

Likewise, our family has followed their example. We are all fully engaging with Molly. We're also grateful for and proud of our kids' responses to their siblings in such a great time of need. No one has stood back in fear of the pain this will bring them. Everyone who is able has come to meet Molly and to embrace and mourn with Jacob and Rebecca. For two days our families have embraced these wounded souls with a depth of love and emotion that is at the same time heartbreaking and comforting. We are here to help absorb the shock, to blunt the sting, each one carrying a part of the grief load.

I'm watching these family relationships grow stronger as we enter the battle with Jacob and Rebecca. In the early hours and days, they faced a hard choice: Would they trust God? Would they respond in faith to the agony that threatened them? They chose yes, and so have we.

Entering into one another's pain is a choice—a choice to feel that pain, to be broken with them. It is a sacrifice of one's self for the good of another. Remaining aloof, choosing not to engage, is also a choice—a choice of self, a choice of safety over sacrifice. But even for this there is grace. All families are wounded and imperfect. As parents we hope that in a time of need our children will rally for one another, but for those who can't or won't we need to be prepared with forgiveness even as the Father so willingly forgives us.

Our families are flawed. We are all sinful, broken people with unique opinions and preferences. Magnifying our complexities is the dissonance of individual relationships; some siblings naturally get along better than others. It's been that way since birth. But what joy it has been, in the midst of this present sorrow, to see disagreements and differences set aside. Only one thing matters: Molly and her parents, a new little family called to battle the giant enemy of death. How comforting to see this anguish shouldered by all. This collective extended family has become a tall fortress of protection, holding back the winds of despair and providing safety, strength, and courage.

When a family pulls together for one of its own, the music of Heaven can be heard.

I would have despaired unless I had believed that I would see the goodness of the LORD in the land of the living. Wait for the LORD; be strong and let your heart take courage; yes, wait for the LORD. (PSALM 27:13–14 NASB)

"Only we who have been washed in the blood of the Lamb

can both weep and laugh at the same time, and with hearts that

are breaking in pieces scattered all over the floor say

with sincerity and honesty that it is well with my soul."

— GARY J. OLIVER,
who lost both his wife and his twenty-three-year-old
son within two months

Dedicating Our Daughter

Molly was moved on Monday to a private room where we had a door and curtains to shut. It was so nice to have a room where we could talk openly and express our feelings without worrying that we might wake up another baby next to us or bother other parents.

It seemed like our siblings had just arrived and now were already preparing to leave. They were saying their farewells, only their good-byes to Molly were different, the kind that truly meant *"I won't see you again in this life."*

That's why what happened next was so important. The day before Jacob had mentioned to me and his mom that he would like to have a dedication service for

Molly. I was so proud of my husband's leadership. He sincerely wanted to consecrate her life to the Lord, whether she lived or not. So Jacob and I decided to have this ceremony with all our family present before our siblings had to leave.

My dad opened the service, reading several psalms and talking about our little Molly girl. As he did, Jacob's dad moved quietly around the room, soothing wounded souls and lifting hurting hearts with his gentle hugs. I held Molly in my arms, seated near her bed while everyone else gathered around us. We had the curtain to Molly's room drawn, and I heard later that there was a buzz around the hospital. The nurses were coming around to listen as the news had spread that we were having a ceremony for Molly. I have no doubt that they became witnesses of our faith in God.

We committed Molly's life to the Lord right there. We asked for God to be honored and glorified through all that was happening in her life and in ours. I felt incredibly grateful to have so many in our family surrounding us. Sitting there in the middle of the room, I was in awe. I wanted time to stand still. I had our daughter in my arms, Jacob at my side, and our family surrounding us.

After a few more scripture readings, we began singing a few songs. Everyone gathered closer around us. Those who were nearest laid their hands on our shoulders or sat by our feet. Some wept and some just stood in silence as Jacob's dad prayed over the three of us. After it was over, those who had to leave came and wept as they said good-bye to Molly and to us. Some whispered in her ear, some just cried as they hugged us and kissed her all over, none wanting to have to leave us or say good-bye to a little girl who had captured their hearts.

After most people left, Samuel, my brother, asked if he could wash Molly's feet. As he was crying so deeply, he used a Kleenex to collect his tears and then wipe Molly's feet gently and with love. He kissed them and whispered something to her. I don't even know what he said, for these were words meant just for Molly.

That was one of many treasured moments.

Later that day, Jacob held Molly in the chair while the two of us processed our feelings and thoughts on whether or not to pursue surgery for Molly. With both sets of parents and my older brother Samuel sitting quietly in the room, Jacob and I talked openly together about what both of us desired for our daughter. Jacob wanted to continue pursuing second opinions while I had decided that if Molly were to die, I wanted us to be with her, holding her close, rather than some doctor who didn't know her or love her like we did. We decided that night not to pursue surgery unless a miracle occurred or some other option became available to us.

Reality kept pressing on us. Just four days into being parents we faced the death of our precious, sweet, amazingly beautiful baby girl.

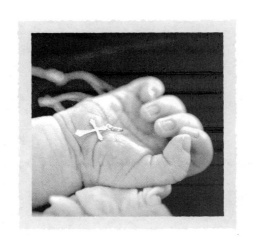

Leaning int

DAY FIVE *Tuesday*

Leaning into Peace

When peace like a river attendeth my way,

when sorrows like sea billows roll;

Whatever my lot, Thou has taught me to say,

"It is well, it is well with my soul."

— HORATIO SPAFFORD,
written after the death of his four
daughters by drowning

Peace

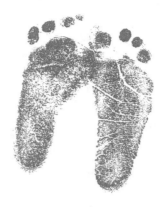

Even though Jacob and Rebecca have made the decision to take Molly off life support, Jacob still has moments of doubt. Today he makes a last stand for his little princess, leaving no stone unturned, no fine print unread.

Understanding her son's heavy heart, Pam says to Dennis and me, "One of the gifts of parenting is helping our children swim through deep waters." So to help confirm the decision, the two grandfathers and Jacob's sister, Lori, who is a nurse, get busy on their phones. So far they have called Arkansas Children's Hospital,

Indiana University Hospital, Johns Hopkins, Mayo Clinic, and several doctors they either know directly or have come across by referral. The questions they ask include: *Is removing life support the right thing to do? Should we try the surgeries? Is there any new procedure we should consider?*

Later, we gather in Molly's room and play "Untitled Hymn" by Chris Rice, a favorite song for many of us. We've listened to it numerous times before, but today it is profoundly more meaningful. Singing along, we come to the words, "Fly to Jesus and live." Our hearts break and we shed what seems like rivers of tears. As the music fades and our sniffles subside, Pam and Bill read a story to Molly that Pam wrote about their six-month-old son who died. Again we cry together. With each experience we feel as if there can't possibly be any more tears, but they keep coming. And we know there are more days of agony ahead. We sometimes feel that this journey is too difficult, that we will not survive it. Yet the hope of Christ, the strong presence of the Holy Spirit in our hearts, and the prayers of thousands give us strength. We sense again that we are in a holy place, nearer still with each day to the orchestra hall of Heaven. We wish we could go with Molly and all be together in a better place.

But we are still firmly rooted to earth. And, not surprisingly, the stress of spending twelve-hour days at the hospital is starting to build up. Each of us feels the fatigue that mourning brings, the weariness of keeping vigil.

Dennis writes about this in an e-mail update to family and friends:

For me, today has been the fifth day in a row of nonstop, God moments—emotionally charged moments that have demanded that we be all here. Yet being here has felt woefully inadequate.

The daddy and Papa part of me has been most relentless. When I've not been in the room with Jake and Rebecca, kissing and stroking Molly, weeping, mostly listening and just being there, I've been helping take care of everything from getting lunch and dinner meals for all seven of us, providing pastoral care since the kids' church pastor is out of town, making trips to the airport and back and comforting all our other children who have been in here at one time or another. All this while I feel my own deep hurt and grief. I cannot imagine going through something like this with a family other than Jake's. Opportunities for the enemy abound in a situation like this. Different families grieve differently.

There is so much emotion wrapped up in this. Deep hurt. I'm grateful for the Mutz family's strong faith and trust in God.

Pray for Jake and Rebecca as they continue to move toward the removal of life support. Their hearts are broken. Scripture tells us our days are numbered. Molly's little life may be comprised of less than seven days.

The other "papas" in our families are feeling the strain too. Jacob, who loves the outdoors and does not do well sitting for long periods of time, needed to get out of the hospital at one point for a brief walk. He needed fresh air and a chance to think by himself.

His father, Bill, was waiting for him upon his return. They walked back together to Molly's room.

"How are you holding up?" Bill asked.

"Part of me is in perfect peace," Jacob said, "and part of me is in despair and denial."

"That's to be expected," Bill reassured. Father and son were quiet a few moments, then Bill added, "Lean into the perfect peace because that is of God."

That's great advice for the rest of us too. We all feel the struggle between peace and denial. To lean into the peace is to surrender to God and His ways.

There is no hope in any other.

When Conflicts Arise

Manhood and womanhood are the beautiful handiwork of a good and loving God.[1]

— JOHN PIPER

One of the most profound realizations I've discovered during this week has been through contrast. Out of all the babies in the NICU, only one other is attended by such a chorus of worshippers. Two disclaimers are needed: (1) some of these babies are not in life-threatening situations as Molly is, and

(2) few of these babies entered the world with such large extended families. The Raineys gave Molly eleven aunts and uncles and twelve cousins, while the Mutzes gave her fourteen aunts and uncles and three cousins! Advantage, Molly!

Next door to Molly is a baby who is fed every four hours by a nurse. Only once in three days have I seen a father or mother in the room with him. The rest of the time this helpless infant is alone. Other babies seem to have family members wandering in and out, always in an aloof, detached sort of way. Most interesting is the absence of men.

In our crisis we are blessed to have not one, but two fathers who have stepped in to provide wise, loving leadership. Grandpa Bill and Papa Rainey listen well to their children, Jacob and Rebecca, and eagerly seek ways to help them. Both men have spent many hours on their laptops and cell phones, helping to find additional information about Molly's condition. They sit in on the meetings with the doctors—as requested by their children—and provide another set of ears for absorbing difficult and complex news. They ask helpful questions that Jacob and Rebecca cannot think of in their state of shock, and they offer their shoulders for comfort.

Benevolent leadership is a foundational need during these difficult days. That need has become evident as our two families' collective vulnerabilities threaten to divide us at a time when we very much need one another. As the stress of long days, the approach of death, and the differences in personalities and preferences have added up, we have begun to experience moments of tension in our relationships. Though our families have many similar values in our Christian faith, we are made up of unique individuals who handle life differently. Not surprisingly, we have unintentionally said and done some hurtful things.

Dennis and Bill, our patriarchs, have decided that it is time for a mid-course correction.

The two of them meet in a small conference room adjacent to the waiting room. They discuss who is feeling what and evaluate what can be done to help our families pull together in providing Jacob and Rebecca what they need.

One concern is that Jacob and Rebecca aren't communicating as well as they were a few days ago. They hardly know what day it is, much less what they need. Plus, they aren't always in Molly's room at the same time. At times there are just too many people coming and going, constantly interrupting their relationship. Honestly, part of their not communicating well is our fault as parents.

Jacob has been leaning heavily on his dad and Dennis. He has needed and wanted their advice and counsel as he has sought so desperately for a solution for Molly. We have gravitated to the pattern of the men helping Jacob and the women helping Rebecca.

I am seeing that I have been in hyper-mother mode. My obsession has been to care for my daughter. Meeting her every desire has been my goal, and I haven't been giving any thought to whether I was offending anyone. (I had no intention to offend, but my focus has been only on meeting Rebecca's needs.) I've been taking care of my girl. If she wants the room cleared, fine. I'll get everyone out to the hallway. If she wants certain family members with her, I'll go get them. Her wish has been my command.

So during their discussion, Dennis and Bill determine that our families will go through this together and we will not become divided. Our primary goal will be to help Jacob and Rebecca communicate better and not to be distracted by all of us. Later,

Pam and I join our husbands. We talk things through a bit more, and then we pray.

I have to say, it has been painful for me to recognize that my protective actions have been detrimental. I cannot save Molly, but out of love for my daughter I wanted to spare her every other pain possible. Acknowledging that my desire to be protective of Rebecca has caused problems is difficult to assimilate. My intentions were good, but in my focus on Rebecca I've not seen how my actions affect others. My personal level of agony and loss increases as I hear God's call to my heart to let go. It is difficult but necessary to become smaller in my role. Oh, how I wish I was sinless. I didn't want to make an already difficult situation harder by offending, and neither did anyone else.

We have changed, today, from being two independent families to one united family, committed to helping both our children. We hadn't realized that prior to this conversation we were operating as two separate units. Pam and I, but especially me, could not be objective enough to see what was really happening; we have been too immersed in the emotion of the crisis. But men can more easily set their emotions aside, see what adjustments are needed, and lead forward.

Bill and Dennis have become a two-man team. They are working together to make sure Jacob and Rebecca are both in the room when new information comes from a nurse or doctor. If something comes up that requires a decision about Molly, Bill and Dennis insist on waiting until both Jacob and Rebecca are present to hear it. They are also making sure that any discussions about the funeral, burial, or memorial include both Jacob and Rebecca and that Pam and I know what is going on if we aren't there when it's discussed. They are coordinating every effort and delegating what they can.

The wonderful benefit to the leadership of these two patriarchs is that we all, wives and children, know they will come to good solutions. We gladly trust their loving, caring initiatives, knowing they have the good of all as their goal. And honestly their team work has relieved some of the stress we have all been feeling.

This experience has reminded me of the definition of manhood that John Piper wrote in his book, *What's the Difference?*:

> The call to leadership for men is not a call to exalt ourselves over any woman [or child]. It is not a call to

domineer or belittle or put women [and children] in their places. They are, after all, fellow-heirs of God and destined for a glory. The call to leadership is a call to humble oneself and take responsibility to be a servant-leader in ways that are appropriate to every different relationship to women [and children].[2]

We have the privilege to walk this dark road with another family who has great faith, and both grandfathers are able to be present during these difficult days, even though they are each keeping up with responsibilities at work via laptops and cell phones. But in taking this journey together we see the inestimable value of mature, wise, male leadership. Without the courage and love of Dennis and Bill, our experience would not be as sweet and bonding as it has become.

God, in His great wisdom created men to lead, to provide for and to protect women and children. I'm seeing clearly this week it is to our advantage as women to recognize this and allow men to lead as God designed for our good, both in times of crisis and in times of normal daily living.

"*Grief is hard work and exhausting. Only with the prayers of others and the minute by minute comfort of the Holy Spirit—even when not felt—can a parent endure the loss of a child.*"

— LYNN STROUD,
mother of seven-year-old Jennifer
who died of cancer

A Day of Dimness

By noon, most of our siblings had gone. It was a letdown of sorts. Having said good-bye all day Monday, we now had to face the fact that time was getting shorter with our little girl. The joy of introducing Molly to her family had ended, and we now had to make difficult decisions in regard to her funeral and memorial service. Her death was imminent. I moved a little numbly, looking for any time to hold Molly, kiss her, or take her picture. We felt a sense of dread at what we knew was about to happen. But we were also bewildered at the immensity of the unknown ahead of us.

We had decided on Monday night that we'd remove life support on Thursday when Molly's nurse, Beth, whom we loved immediately, would be back on duty. My biggest reason for removing life support was a selfish one. I wanted to be with her when she met Jesus. I wanted Jacob and me to be the ones who held her as she was ushered into the King's presence. Neither of us wanted her on a surgeon's table as her little life slipped away.

There was a piece of Jacob that still hadn't given up finding a solution. He still clung to any small shred of hope that presented itself. He, along with all of us, wanted a miracle or some doctor to come forward with a breakthrough treatment or skill that would end our suffering.

No such doctor existed, and no breakthrough treatment surfaced, though Jacob searched high and low and called nearly every children's hospital in the country. He even had her medical records sent to several hospitals and was waiting for their opinions as late as Thursday morning. He valiantly searched for a way, any way, to save his dear little princess. He wanted no regrets as a daddy.

There was something about this day, Tuesday, that makes it a blur in my memory. For the past four days we'd been overwhelmed with visitors and family coming, which we loved and needed, but we'd also been crushed by the meetings with doctors and nurses giving nothing but bad news. We were left wearied and worn and weakened. No one new would be coming to see Molly anymore.

The music was deep and dark.

The end was near.

The

Master

Comes

The Master Comes

"*Suppose you are a gardener employed by another; it is not your garden,*

but you are called upon to tend it . . . You come one morning into the garden,

and you find that the best rose has been taken away. You are angry;

you go to your fellow servants, and charge them with having taken the rose.

They will declare that they had nothing at all to do with it; and one says,

'I saw the master walking here this morning; I think he took it'

Is the gardener angry then? No, at once he says, 'I am happy that my rose should

have been so fair as to attract the attention of the master.

It is his own: he hath taken it; let him do what seemeth him good.'"

It is even so with your friends. They wither not by chance;

the grave is not filled by accident; men die according to God's will.

Your child is gone, but the Master took it; your husband is gone, your wife buried—

the Master took them; thank him that he let you have the pleasure

of caring for them and tending them while they were here,

and thank him that as he gave, he Himself has taken away. [1]

— CHARLES SPURGEON

Treasures in

th

Treasures in the Darkness

He [the Christian believer] can say, "If I should lose all I have, it is better that I should lose than have if God so wills: the worst calamity is the wisest and the kindest thing that could befall me if God ordains it." "We know that all things work together for good to them that love God."

— CHARLES SPURGEON

Darkness

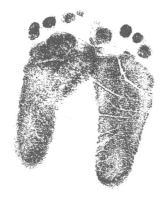

How do you spend what could be your last full day on earth with your child?

Jacob and Rebecca choose to do the ordinary things that parents might do with a newborn, things that in this circumstance become extraordinary. The urgency has increased to capture more moments with Molly, to savor her presence more intensely, to create more first-time experiences. We are keenly aware that whatever "firsts" we have this day will be the one, the only, the last.

The video camera is on and several digital cameras are in near-constant use. Rebecca and Jacob give Molly her first and only bath, gently and tenderly washing her hair. This is the first time they have held her precious little naked body, and they inhale her sweet scent. A simple bath, but it is quietly symbolic of the Word of God which washes all who believe in Christ. This lovely and holy preparation readies Molly to greet her King. There is a hush in the room. She is being anointed for her debut into heavenly worship. Her cleansing is a faint echo of His music, His symphony of redemption from before the dawn of time.

Then Molly is again diapered and snuggled in her soft pink blanket, sleeping peacefully in her little bed.

Afterward a nurse brings in an ink pad to get Molly's footprints and handprints. At first the nurse dutifully makes the prints on ordinary paper, but Dennis asks if he can have Molly's footprints in his Bible. The nurse agrees, which inspires each of us to grab our Bibles to preserve a print of Molly's little life. Rebecca finds her red journal that she kept all through her pregnancy and has both of Molly's footprints and her left handprint preserved in the front. Molly sleeps through most of this, untroubled that her footprints are now all over Psalm 127—where the psalmist writes about children being a gift from the Lord—or that her left handprint is next to her Papa's life verse, Psalm 112:1–2: "Praise the LORD! Blessed is the man who fears the LORD, who greatly delights in his commandments! His offspring will be mighty in the land; the generation of the upright will be blessed."

Mighty Molly is now her new name.

There is a sweet reverence as we capture these treasures and remembrances. That night, after we leave the hospital, Jacob and Rebecca are alone again with Molly. About 10:00 p.m. family and friends receive this e-mail from Jacob:

> *I just got done holding Molly chest to chest for the last three and a half hours! Heavenly. I could feel her beating heart on my bare chest. Molly is an angel; 2,569 kisses later I relinquished her to Mom. Now Rebecca is experiencing this delight! I just looked over at Bec and she nodded, as if to say, I will be sleeping here with my Sweet Pea for the next twelve hours.*

Why Every Life Matters

Among all God's creatures, only humanity receives the image of God, and that quality separates us from all else ... God's image is

*not an arrangement of skin cells or a physical shape, but rather an
inbreathed Spirit.*[1]

— DR. PAUL BRAND AND PHILIP YANCEY

A tiny helpless babe. One unable to make a sound, to give a smile, to even take a breath on her own.

Newborns are dependent on others for the sustenance of life. Someone else must feed, clothe, and clean them. Newborns can do none of these life tasks on their own, but most have the potential to develop to independence.

Molly is different.

She has no potential for an independent life. The news from the doctors makes it clear that her brain damage renders her unable to be a normal child or for her body systems to sustain life. So what is her life worth? What meaning does her little life have?

In this era of genetic testing and technology, expectant parents face choices unheard of in previous generations. For centuries, pregnancy has been a time of mystery, surprise, and sometimes apprehension and fear—especially in generations past when many infants and mothers died at birth. Medical advances have brought both life-saving discoveries and life-ending detections.

If Jacob and Rebecca had known about Molly's condition before her birth, would that have made it easier?

Some might wonder. But it's doubtful. The mourning would have only begun sooner. Would they have been less attached? Impossible. The mother-child attachment is part of the relationship inherent in God's design for babies growing inside a mother's womb. God asks the rhetorical question in Isaiah 49:15: "Can a woman forget her nursing child, that she should have no compassion on the son of her womb?"

Molly's life began at conception, and her parents have had the privilege of enjoying her for nine months and one week in utero. Because there was no suspicion of anything wrong, no testing was offered and none was done. Rebecca and Jacob enjoyed the journey of pregnancy.

We have always believed, and still do, that life is a gift given by God. He is the Creator, the Author, the Originator—"Thus says the LORD, your Redeemer, who formed you from the womb: I am the LORD, who made all things" (Isaiah 44:24a). We also believe that God says human life has value because we are created in His image, in His likeness. Everything about us is a reflection of Him, the Trinity, the Three in One.

Molly is God's little image bearer, and her life has been carefully crafted by Him for His glory. It does not matter to God that Molly's body is not whole. He made her that way; her life is not an accident. To say that her malformations were a fluke or a random mutation is to say that her development was outside of God's control. He forms and fashions His living image bearers with heavenly and eternal purposes in mind. And He loves each one passionately.

The purpose of Molly's life is no less important than that of David, king of Israel, of whom it was said, "After he had served the purpose of God in his own generation, fell asleep" (Acts 13:36). We do not know the purposes God conceived when He made Molly, but we can guess at what some of them might be. We know that her life has invited us to give thanks and praise to

God. She has focused our attention on Heaven, reminding us of the eternal and that none of us knows how much time we have on earth. In the small bounds of her fragile life an entire world of meaning and dignity has been revealed to those who have come near—a glimpse of eternity, a touch of the holy, a melodious chorus of Heaven.

I am also convinced there are purposes for Molly's life that we will not know until Heaven. God will continue using her life even after she is gone from here. There are deep mysteries in the mind of God that are too wonderful for us to know, too high for us to grasp.

My son, Samuel, said it well in an e-mail he sent to family and friends:

> *Truly her life has been extraordinary. If there was a symbol that gives you a picture of her life, it is the exclamation point! She came, she changed, and now she is going. Molly's work here on earth is done, and what an amazing work she has done. In seven days, she has accomplished more than most 77-year-olds. I pray that you experience the ripple, nay, the waves of change that her life has caused.*

Molly herself was made for worship, as it says in Psalm 8:2 (NIV), "From the lips of children and infants you have ordained praise," and she was given to her parents that they might worship the King. May you also feel the touch of the Master's hand, hear the song of the Creator's call, and give praise to God for all He does.

"Mom, you think too much. God sent His Son to die for me!

If God never answered another prayer of mine,

if He doesn't heal me, if I have brain tumors and suffer,

no matter what happens to me, sending His Son for me is enough.

So, Mom, just focus on that, praise Him for sending Jesus,

and quit worrying about the tumors."

— THOMAS EPTING, 16,
spoken one month before he died from inoperable brain cancer

A Simple
Sweetness

Such a beautiful day. We didn't think of the ticking clock or how the time was ebbing away. We focused all we had on Molly.

This was the day we got to give her a bath. A bath may seem like such a small, insignificant thing, but for us it became like a treasured jewel. The memory of this is so dear to Jacob and me, something we hold close to our hearts.

It had been bothering me all week that Molly still had tiny bits of dried blood from birth in her hair. From those first few minutes after birth, when it became clear that things weren't quite right, the nurses stopped working on cleaning her up. They whisked her away to get her on oxygen.

I had tried, every chance I got, to get out as much of the blood in her hair as I could, but there was only so much I could do. I knew warm water and soap would do the trick. We laid her on several soft towels, still on her bed, and gently washed her from head to toe. I wanted her hair to be clean and smooth so that we might brush it and see more of its beauty.

As our parents and Lori and Kelli watched from behind the lenses of cameras or over our shoulders, we gently washed Molly's skin and gave her a clean look. She didn't care too much for having her hair washed, but once we gently rolled her on her stomach she quieted down and fell into a deep sleep. We all gazed in awe at her precious little back. Jacob and I gently washed it, too, taking note of her sweet cutie buns! They were so little and almost nonexistent, but they still got plenty of kisses. For some reason, Molly's back smelled like peppermint to me. No one else got the scent, but I did, sweet and fresh.

Giving Molly a bath was so fulfilling, so memorable. As a mom, I wanted to take care of our little girl. For most of the week I felt helpless to give our baby what she needed. There was always a nurse to change her diaper or move her from side to side or change her feeding drip. It was so wonderful, such a cherished moment, that we, her parents, were able to care for her. When she didn't like some of it, I would whisper in her ear and speak loving words that calmed her little heart. Jacob even loved brushing her dark brown hair. Neither of us will ever forget those moments of bathing our daughter, as we dressed her for her meeting with her King.

That night after everyone left, Jacob and I snuggled up with our little Molly girl and held her close once more. Jacob would have held her longer had I not protested that it was my turn. Oh, what a joy it was to hold her so near. As most newborns do, she slept a lot but I think she slept better when she was in our arms and close to our hearts. It's where she belonged, no matter what was wrong with her. She was safe with us. It was heavenly having her in our arms, lying against our chests, feeling her heart beating. Her little hands brushed against my skin as she slept soundly and comfortably.

We held her like that until well after midnight, finally relinquishing her to her own bed so that we could get some rest. That night, we slept on the couch in her room, not caring about the beeps or nurses coming and going, just that we were close to our Molly girl.

Coronation

Coronation Day

If God hides the reason for His works from us, and it is too high for us to reach, let us shut our mouths; . . . let us glorify God and not be ashamed to be ignorant. The true wisdom of the faithful is to know no more than it has pleased God to show them.

— JOHN CALVIN

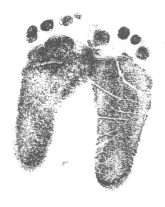

At dawn, while watching the Colorado sunrise, Dennis writes an e-mail to friends and colleagues:

The Son will soon be welcoming home Rebecca and Jake's daughter, Molly,

a gift entrusted to them for seven days, to be ushered home undoubtedly

by a band of the gentlest angels dispatched from the throne of God

to carry her into the presence of the Savior.

Ecclesiastes 7:1–2 (NASB) says,

"The day of one's death is better than the day of one's birth.

It is better to go to a house of mourning

Than to go to a house of feasting,

Because that is the end of every man,

And the living takes it to heart."

Our hearts are breaking.

These seven days have been so full of the presence of God, honoring Him for Molly Ann. And now today is our last day, the day of Molly's death. But it is also Molly's Coronation Day. This morning we will say good-bye, one by one, and then leave Rebecca and Jacob to spend the afternoon alone with their baby. Molly is expected to live only a few minutes after being taken off life support.

Arriving at the hospital, we are greeted with a report of Molly's condition overnight. I then ask Rebecca the same questions I've been asking every morning: *Have you slept? Did either of you eat? Have you pumped? Do you need anything?*

Soon we are consumed with the details of death. Some decisions and arrangements still have to be made. We begin moving belongings out of the room Rebecca and Jacob have occupied; we don't want to be distracted by mundane necessities at the end. There is some redemption in the monotony of these tasks. Perhaps these duties keep us from imploding; perhaps they simply give us a feeling of momentary purpose.

E-mails and text messages begin filling our voicemail and inboxes. At 10:00 a.m. Samuel Rainey writes:

> *I keep shaking my head at the thought of what Jake and Rebecca have to do today. The decision they made on Monday not to pursue surgery was difficult to say the least, but the decision facing them today is incomprehensible. Today they have to let Molly go, end her suffering by taking her off life support. They are sending her to Jesus. There are no words, just my shaking head.*

At 12:30, the leaving begins. Beth, Molly's nurse, tells us that Molly is ready to go. Her heart rate is up significantly since yesterday. She's on more oxygen and her saturation level is lower. She is turning blue.

At 12:44, Ben Rainey sends a message from the waiting room at Children's Hospital to friends:

We're about to say our good-byes to little Molly. It's much harder than I thought it would be. Life shouldn't be like this. Life shouldn't hurt this much. My heart is a mess. It took me around thirty minutes to type this on my Blackberry because it's hard to find the keys through my tears. And while we weep here with them, her little broken body will be instantly healed. In a flash, she will be with the Creator of the universe, the One who created her, and our souls rest in this. We take comfort that we will see her again.

At 1:00 p.m., Rebecca and Jacob make a very selfless decision. They want the four grandparents to get to hold Molly. None of us expected this gift. We had never even asked as we didn't want to rob them of one minute with their sweet daughter. So up until this point nobody has held Molly except Jacob and Rebecca. I hold Molly first and it is quite a maneuver to make sure all the wires and tubes supporting her life don't get tangled. But finally she is in my arms, Mimi's granddaughter. I hold her close and coo words of love and admiration over her beautiful face. Smiles and tears mingle. I don't want to take my hands off her. It is heartbreaking to hold Molly the first time, knowing this will be the last time.

Next it is Pam's turn and then Bill's. Pam rocks gently and sings "Jesus Loves Me." Watching them with her is a joy, especially Bill who has the most tender heart. He kisses her and tells her some of his favorite verses. They kiss on her some more and cry as they say good-bye.

Last is Dennis' turn. Jacob says, "Tell her a story, Papa. Tell her a Speck story!" Rebecca gets a huge grin on her face at the idea and chimes in, "Oh yes, Dad, please tell her a Speck story!"

Speck stories began when our children were little, and now Dennis has started telling the grandkids these adventure stories of tiny little people and tiny little creatures who live in a make-believe, microscopic world. There they face any number of challenges that demand courage and faith. Our kids have been enthralled with these tiny people stories that take the Speck children to the very edge of danger. And no matter what, the story always ends the same: "And you'll have to wait until tomorrow night to hear the rest of the story."

Molly's Speck story is about a Speck Papa and a Speck Grand-daughter who go fishing one day together. "They caught their tiny

Speck fish and were going to eat their fish when they encountered something you will never believe . . . and you'll have to wait until I join you in Heaven to hear the rest of the story." Dennis is crying so much between each phrase that the story begins and ends in three sentences.

We are all crying, but Rebecca is beaming. And then she and Jacob start laughing at the way Dennis blubbered through the last line. It's so pitiful that we all start laughing. For several seconds we can't stop. Dennis looks up at Molly's monitors, afraid that his laughing was shaking her and stressing her system when we all see, to our great surprise, that Molly's oxygen rate is on the rise. It's been at 80 all day, now it hits 90, then 92, then 93, 94, 95, 98, 99 . . . 100! We cheer like we're at a football game. Molly's oxygen rate hasn't reached 100 in more than 24 hours.

We ask Beth about it, and she shrugs her shoulders. "I don't know how that happened," she says. "I've never seen anything like it before."

Rebecca said, "I think that was God was showing us, 'I could do this if I really wanted. I could heal her right now. I would be honored in her life and her death and I could heal her if I wanted to, but I'm not. It's not my purpose for her or you.'"

It is one of those moments that only God can give in the middle of deep anguish. We know this is the last time we are going to see Molly alive and we are so sad, and yet God gives us joy in the middle of our grief. This moment was the crescendo in the symphony, a glorious sound of victory riding over the rumble of death. "It was sheer delight and mystery," Dennis wrote later. "A small thing, perhaps, but in the valley of the shadow of death, God gave us a visible touch of His presence. He was smiling and laughing with us."

Now Rebecca is holding Molly again and the laughter has stopped. Dennis and I kneel beside her as he reads a good-bye letter to Molly:

My Dearest Mighty Molly,

I just met you—I feel cheated. I don't want to say good-bye. I know I'll likely see you in a couple of decades or so—in light of eternity, it won't be long, really. Still, I don't want to say good-bye. You will always be my Molly, my granddaughter.

I'm really sad that I won't be getting to spoil you with a doll, or go sneak chocolate, or take you on ice cream dates, and eat chocolate pie and pudding, laughing all the time at what your mommy and daddy would say if they knew what we were doing.

Your seven days sure brought a lot of joy to your mom's and dad's faces—I've watched them drink you in with their eyes, kiss you from head to foot, stroke and caress you. Your parents loved you well. God couldn't have given you better parents. Courageous parents. They have loved you with a sacrificial love that only a very few little girls like you ever get to experience. It hurts their hearts so much.

Oh, how I really don't want to say good-bye.

Sweet Molly, until that day in Heaven, when we will celebrate the greatness of our God together (then we will go sneak chocolate and go on an ice cream date), I must say good-bye.

Good-bye, Molly Ann.

I love you,

Papa

The time has come for Jacob and Rebecca to be alone with Molly. The four of us leave and walk down the hall. I can hardly walk a straight line because of the burden of grief. Out in the waiting room we sit and cry.

After a time, we pick up our laptops and start writing again—to our children first, to tell them all about holding Molly, and then to friends who are e-mailing their prayers for us at this moment. Our children are in their usual places—Samuel in class at grad school, Laura and Deborah both at work, Ashley at a family reunion—but their hearts were in the NICU unit of Children's Hospital. Emotionally we are together waiting for the end. They want to be in touch, to experience every minute with us.

At 3:00 p.m., Samuel writes: *My Old Testament class has been praying for Molly, Jake, and Bec each day this week. Today, many of my friends have dressed in black; adorned in support of Molly and the Mutz family. They also brought flowers and a candle and placed them at the front of the class, ever beckoning all 130 students to remember, to pray, and to be blessed by the life of Molly Ann Mutz.*

At 4:37 Lori Mutz Alt, who is with us in the waiting room, writes:

I just talked to Jake. They will give the word to remove the tubes soon.

At 4:40 Laura Rainey writes: *Oh noooooooooooooo. Will you call me?*

Then Samuel again at 4:42: *I cannot fathom. Simply cannot.*

We've been sitting in the waiting room for several hours. The longer we wait, the greater my anxiety grows. My heart is aching to be near my child. I want to run to Rebecca, scoop her up, and take her away. I want to carry her to bed, tuck her in tight, and tell her it will be all right. But I can't rescue my baby girl from this valley of the shadow of death any more than she can rescue her baby girl from certain death. My stomach is full of . . . not butterflies—that's too gentle—it's crawling and twisting with fear for my daughter and her husband. Will they survive this? Will Molly have pain? How long will she last? It is agony.

The clock on the wall seems to creep.

At 5:30 Samuel e-mails: *Quivering.*

More e-mails that ask, "Is she gone?" "How are they?" and "What's happening?"

Sitting in the waiting room I feel so distant from Molly who is at the end of a long hallway. I want to be near, for the kids to know we are here. They seem so far away.

Just after 6:00 we get the message that the life support has been removed. Soon, Beth appears at the door saying, "I think Rebecca needs you." I jump up and run, meeting Rebecca in the hallway. She had left the room and was crying. "I just can't do it anymore. I can't be there anymore, I can't stay there. Molly's gasping. They say she's not in pain, and they say she's not suffering, but she's gone, Mom. She's gone."

I pull Rebecca to me and wrap my arms around her. We stand in the hall for a few minutes, crying together, and then she says, "Let's go back and watch through the window." We walk back, and stand tightly together, watching Jacob hold Molly. He is sitting in the shadows, the window behind him, facing our direction. Sweet Molly is cradled in his arms, resting on his knees. All we can see is the top of his head as he continues to gaze at his precious lifeless baby.

After a couple minutes, Beth checks on Jacob, and he asks for his mom. Dennis and Bill come, too, and stand next to Rebecca and me while Pam goes in to sit with Jacob. After ten minutes or so, Rebecca goes back in and sits beside them. She then motions for all of us to come back in.

Oh, sweet Molly. I wasn't prepared to see her beautiful body without life. I feel a deep groan in my soul as I see her drained of color and life. She is gone. I sobbed as quietly as I could, but, oh, I felt like wailing. I miss her so already.

We wait with them in the darkening room until about 7:45 when Rebecca says she is ready to leave. They'd been holding Molly's body for nearly two hours and though she wanted to stay with her forever, she knew she couldn't. Jacob says that he's not ready to go yet, and they agree that he will stay and hold Molly a little longer. As we drive away from the hospital, thunderstorms have blown up over the mountains. A dazzling sunset splashed platinum gold shafts of light all over the Rockies. The light behind the clouds is brilliant, as though the sun was declaring, "Magnificent Molly is home!"

Dennis captured the moment in an e-mail to family and friends:

> Molly's last day with us began with a pretty average sunrise, but the sunset that closed out her Coronation Day was spectacular.

The Scriptures declare, "This is the day the Lord has made, let us rejoice and be glad in it." That verse challenged our faith all day long, but it was nonetheless a day ordered by God's sovereign hand of love and mercy for calling Molly home.

Back at the hospital, Jacob was struggling to let go. He continued to hold Molly until finally Bill and Pam went in to bring him out. When Jacob came down to the hospital lobby, Lori said what was left of her heart shattered at the sight of him walking slowly with slumped shoulders, his head down. She took his face in her hands and looked in his eyes and said, "Do you know that what you just did was the most protecting thing you could do for your little girl?" He shook his head no. He had tears in his eyes. She told him again, "Do you know that what you just did shows that you love your little girl with selfless love?" Again he shook his head no. "Jacob," she said, "you are being the best dad imaginable. You chose to be selfless so that your little girl would not have to suffer. I am so proud of you."

He looked at Lori and said, "Tell me that every month."

As we reflect on the testimony of Molly's mighty, magnificent life, we see it as a tribute to the two people who brought her into this world and who loved her so very well. Her death is a testimony to the power of God in a life. Having known my daughter for twenty-eight years, I thought she would collapse under the weight of this great loss, but she has stood firmly on a foundation that will not move. The power of God in her life is stunning to me. And it has been equally true of Jacob. They have built their house on the rock, as it says in Matthew 7:24–25, "Everyone then who hears these words of mine and does them will be like a wise man who built his house on the rock. And the rain fell, and the floods came, and the winds blew and beat on that house, but it did not fall, because it had been founded on the rock."

Rebecca and Jacob did not fall that day. They felt deeply the fury of the winds and the rain, but in the end they survived the storm stronger than they were before.

And we who are family have had the great privilege to walk this dark path with them, to be touched by Molly, to encounter the living God who was, and is, so near.

Why Faith Is the Victory

To believe in Christ, in this moment, in this perplexity, in this frustration, in these setbacks, in this present agony, is victory of the highest order.[1]

— ANDRÉE SEU

Our e-mail updates and blog posts became viral, and thousands have been praying and sending comments. One of the most repeated comments we've heard during the week of Molly's life and after is a sincere acknowledgement of self-doubt: "I don't know if I could handle this the way Jacob and Rebecca have."

Watching from outside often leads the observer to ponder what his or her own response might be. From a vantage point of relative peace and calm, seeing others battle cancer or divorce or some other kind of loss can threaten our own sense of confidence. We wonder what our response would be to something that appears too difficult to endure.

From watching Jacob and Rebecca during the week, I have learned that we can have complete confidence in God's power to strengthen those who belong to him. The answer to the question, "Could I do this?" is a resounding yes! If you belong to Him.

I can do all things through him [Christ] who strengthens me. (PHILIPPIANS 4:13)

And my God will supply every need of yours

according to his riches in glory in Christ Jesus.

(PHILIPPIANS 4:19)

But he said to me, "My grace is sufficient for you,

for my power is made perfect in weakness."

(2 CORINTHIANS 12:9)

How real these truths have become to me, seeing God's Spirit
strengthen my child beyond what I could have imagined. God has
worked a wonder in her broken heart. She is a testimony to me of
the power of God moving in a life. She and Jacob have been
walking through this by faith, believing in the goodness of God.

Another wondrous experience of this week has been the almost
tangible presence of God. He has been at work in our hearts. As
Christians we are prone to regard only physical healings or super-
natural occurrences as genuine works of God. But the restorative
change of a broken human heart is truly the greatest miracle of
all. God performed many of these miracles during Molly's time
with us as we cooperated with Him by believing in Him.

It is by faith that God works, Hebrews 11:6 reminds us, "And without faith it is impossible to please him." Yet we mistakenly assume that faith is the means to an end, or conclude that if we had more faith we could move mountains and Molly could have been healed. But is God controlled by our faith? Must He move at our request if we present the correct amount of faith to Him? Or did He want to heal Molly but couldn't because we didn't ask enough or believe strongly enough? No. Faith is the victory, not the miracle. First John 5:4 tells us, "And this is the victory that has overcome the world—our faith." Spanning thirty-five verses, Hebrews 11 tells us of great deeds done by faith, but there is a shift in verse 36, which says with pronounced contrast that "others suffered." The writer adds to the previous list of heroic deeds a new list that includes mockings, imprisonment, destitution, affliction, and death.

Along with Jacob and Rebecca, our family has joined the chorus of the Bible's faithful in performing acts of faith. Our deeds may not qualify as the type in the first part of the list—"conquered kingdoms . . . stopped the mouths of lions . . . escaped the edge of the sword" (Hebrews 11:33–34)—but ours did qualify under God's definition: "Faith is the assurance of things hoped for, the conviction of things not seen" (Hebrews 11:1).

By faith we believe God's word is true, every word of it, and we talk of it daily, and are strengthened by it.

By faith we accepted Molly's life as a good and perfect gift. We believe her days were numbered and ordered by God for great good.

By faith we believe God and choose His way of forgiveness and unity as families.

By faith we believe that the God who called our children to this journey will also give them the strength and courage to walk it.

By faith we believe that Heaven is real, that Molly has been called there and is more alive now than ever.

By faith we believe that God's ways are higher than our ways, that we wouldn't understand if He told us all the reasons for this great sorrow, and that His taking Molly was not a sign that He loved us any less.

By faith we choose to believe Habakkuk 3:17-18:

> Though the fig tree should not blossom,
> nor fruit be on the vines,

the produce of the olive fail

and the fields yield no food,

the flock be cut off from the fold

and there be no herd in the stalls,

yet I will rejoice in the Lord;

I will take joy in the God of my salvation.

Today has been the culmination of Molly Ann's earthly life. For those of us left behind it has been an indescribable day. We stood on the threshold of eternity, touched the hem of Heaven, and worshipped God there, giving thanks for His presence and His gift of Molly Ann Mutz.

"To me seven years was not enough time with Rick, much less having only seven days as you have had with Molly. I do not remember how long it took me not to be sad, but instead to have joy that he was part of my life at all, but it happened. Eternity will be a lot longer than the 60 or 70 years I might have had with him, so even though it was a great loss, in the grand plan the Lord has for us, I know all will be well and someday I will understand."

— JOHN PETERSON,
Rebecca's uncle, whose six-year-old son died in a car wreck

Standing at the Doorway of Heaven

I could feel the end coming. Death was knocking. All I wanted was to hold Molly closely and speak loving words into her ear.

The last of Jacob's siblings had flown in early Thursday morning to meet Molly and say good-bye. They were ushered in one by one, to smile at her, give her kisses, and pose for pictures before they went back to the waiting room.

With each person's hello and good-bye, I was feeling increasingly nervous and scared.

Around 1:00 p.m., we called in the grandparents to give them a final gift of holding Molly close to their hearts as they each said good-bye. When my dad held her and told her a story that he used to tell me as a little girl, I was so proud. My daughter was getting a story time just like I used to get.

After the grandparents had said goodbye, we asked for our photographer. A friend of ours, Heather Lilly, had taken some maternity pictures of me not long before Molly was born. Hearing about Molly's condition, Heather had signed up with the nonprofit Now I Lay Me Down To Sleep, which helps families capture the final photos of a dying newborn or child.

We asked Heather to take our photos in two sessions. The first session was with Molly still attached to all her life supports. In the second session, the tubes would be removed and we would get to hold her closer than ever, since her birth. We wanted pictures of her without the tubes, without all the tape, just pure and beautiful.

As Molly was placed in Jacob's arms, Heather started snapping away. She encouraged us to just love on our daughter, talk to her, kiss her, and gaze at her. I held her hands as she lay in Jacob's lap and we both drank her in, enjoying every curve of her little body. She even opened her eyes for a bit to give us the gift of peering into her little soul, wondering what it was like to be so close to meeting Jesus. Heather took pictures of Molly with Jacob, who was shirtless, so father and daughter were just skin to skin.

After awhile we moved her to her bed and dressed her in a "going home" outfit, which took on a whole new meaning. I had brought a little white dress with just a bit of a ruffle on the sleeve, a summer dress, with white bloomers to go over her diaper—a really simple, really sweet dress, with one little button on the back. Our nurse helped us put the dress on Molly, slipping it over all her tubes. We tied on little pink satin ballet slippers and slipped a gold cross necklace around her neck, gifts from my brother Samuel and his wife Stephanie.

Then we read her some storybooks, The Little Engine That Could and Love You Forever, and we prayed over her. The photographer continued taking pictures the entire time.

Then Molly was put in my arms and Heather continued to take pictures, this time with me holding her all dressed up and looking beautiful. After awhile, Heather slipped out of the room and left us alone with Molly.

I looked at Jacob and we both knew what the other was thinking. How could we do this? How could we let our precious daughter die?

Beth came in and asked us how long we wanted before the tubes came out. Neither of us could give her an answer. How does one decide the time we have with someone when it is our very last? I looked at her with tears in my eyes and told her we didn't *know how long or when we wanted to do it. I asked her to decide for us. I referred*

to the clock and how it seemed to mock us and the short time we had left.

Beth pulled a chair over to the wall and took down the clock. She reassured us.

Take as long as you want. She told us just enjoy Molly.

We nodded and agreed and then she left.

I held Molly, and Jacob sat next to us. We wanted to savor her scent, remember the

feel of her skin beneath our lips, the silkiness of her hair in our fingers, the brightness

of her eyes. Was she seeing more than we could? Was she seeing eternity? We felt all

sorts of emotions as we sat together and loved on our daughter, the child we prayed

for, the one we were sending to Jesus. I don't know how much time passed, but the

next time Beth came in and asked if we were ready, we told her we weren't.

We asked her for a little more time. After she left I cried as we talked about

Molly and how much we loved her. Molly continued to sleep soundly against my

chest, safe and secure. Beth returned maybe twenty minutes later and this time

we didn't say anything. We didn't ask for more time. We just let it happen.

I was still holding Molly, dressed in the purest white and wrapped in a soft green

blanket. I started to cry as Beth came close and gently pulled away the tape from

Molly's cheeks, preparing to remove the tubes and turn off the oxygen. My eyes spilled over with tears. I whispered to Molly, "Sweetie, sweetie, sweetie . . . Mommy loves you. Daddy loves you. Molly, we love you so much!" We asked Jesus to come get her quickly because we didn't want her to suffer, didn't want her to hurt.

When the oxygen was turned off and the tubes were removed, it seemed to be happening in slow motion. All was quiet, except for me who was crying and talking to Molly the entire time.

I stood up with her close to my heart, something I hadn't been able to do all week, and Jacob and I walked over to the couch in her room. As we sat down facing each other, I gently lowered our daughter to my lap and Jacob wrapped his arms around mine as I continued to hold Molly. We held her together and I knew she was gone. I knew it the instant I saw her face. Her color had drained immediately. She was lifeless and still. Her eyes were gently shut and her mouth slightly parted as if she were sleeping. I knew she was with Jesus.

Jacob asked me several times to help him cry. He was so numb, so empty. I continued to sob, unable to help my husband shed tears of sorrow too. Even though I knew Molly was gone, little gasps came from her body, the worst sound I have ever heard. While her soul was being lifted away in the arms of gentle angels, her body continued to fight for life.

My heart broke into pieces, and I wept. I told Jacob how hard it was for me to hear her struggle. Jacob encouraged me to find my mom and wait in the hallway. Jacob took Molly from me and I left the room. He cradled her body on his lap, cleaned the tape residue from her face, and spoke words of love and admiration to her, never taking his eyes off of her.

I ran down the long hallway to my mom, who held me tightly and cried with me as we walked back to Molly's room, arms around each other. We were soon joined by my dad and Jacob's parents, all crying in anguish.

We stood there and cried, and Mom assured me over and over that we had done the right thing. After awhile we all went in together and I held Molly in my arms again, kissing her sweet face, telling her that I loved her.

My heart was heavy, but I knew that Molly was now whole and with Jesus.

Worship

and

Worship and Anguish

Suffering (getting what one does not want while wanting what one does not get) is specified in Scripture as part of every Christian's calling . . .

— J. I. PACKER

Anguish

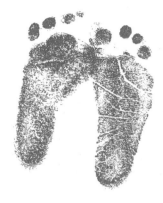

"What do you wear to your newborn daughter's funeral?" Hearing those words sent a stab of pain into my soul. It's a jarring thought, hard to absorb.

Yesterday, our daughter Laura and Rebecca's best friend Christy arrived in Denver. The four of us went to the mall to help Rebecca find something to wear to Molly's funeral. We felt like aliens. Everyone and everything appeared as though suffering and death did not exist on the planet. What store has associates trained to help with our request: "Excuse me, but do you have something my daughter might wear to the burial of her baby girl?"

Simply numbing.

Rebecca eventually settled on a simple, light pink dress that she already had at home. She did not want to wear black.

Today is Saturday, the day of Molly's burial. At the appointed time, the Mutz and Rainey families accompany Jacob and Rebecca to the cemetery. The spot chosen for Molly's burial is in a corner section that is reserved for babies. From there we can see the foothills of the Rocky Mountains.

As we walk toward the green tent flapping in the strong breeze, I am unprepared for the sight of the tiny white casket, slightly larger than a shoe box, waiting for us as we approach. It takes my breath away. The sight of it feels so wrong. Its white ruffles cannot soften the harsh blow of death. All around me I hear soft gasps and sobbing. I see my adult children and their spouses, the Mutz children and spouses, standing in a semicircle with faces that reflect deeply broken hearts.

Incomprehensible.

Dennis and Bill again have the difficult task of leading us to see beyond the grave in front of us. Each one reads Scripture and prays, guiding our eyes and hearts to Jesus, the Resurrected One. They encourage us to believe that though this moment feels too much to bear, God in His great unending love will help us through. They read Psalm 46:1-3:

God is our refuge and strength,

a very present help in trouble.

Therefore we will not fear though the earth gives way,

though the mountains be moved into the heart of the sea,

though its waters roar and foam,

though the mountains tremble at its swelling.

But it does feel, right now, like the earth has shifted beneath us. Standing in this place of death we feel swept away from all that is familiar and normal and predictable. The waves of grief threaten to pull us under. Molly's death has introduced another kind of death to our family, the death of idealism that says if you play by the rules everything will be well.

Dennis closes his portion by reading what will be written on Molly's marker. It's a profound declaration, a rhyme we found on a gravestone next to an old church in England. Buried there was a little family: a mother who died in childbirth, the baby who only lived a few months, and the father who died one year later. I'd taken a photograph of it, never imagining that this little poem would one day mark the grave of a baby in our family.

We cannot Lord
thy purpose see
but all is well
that's done by thee.

The ceremony is brief, and at the end Jacob and Rebecca release a single, pink, helium-filled balloon on which they had written messages to Molly. We quietly leave for the church across the street while Jacob and Rebecca stay with Molly's casket for a few private moments.

The mood inside the church, already filling with family and friends, is somber and hushed. At the front are four large, black and white photographs of Molly and her parents, taken the last day of Molly's life. Rebecca and Jacob wanted everyone to see their beautiful baby girl.

Again, Bill and Dennis lead us in celebrating the life of Molly Ann Mutz, praising God's goodness for giving her to us for seven beautiful days. Sniffing and crying can be heard as we listen to the words of truth and comfort:

The eyes of the LORD are toward the righteous and His ears toward their cry. (PSALM 34:15)

The LORD is near to the brokenhearted and saves the crushed in spirit. (PSALM 34:18)

I praise you, for I am fearfully and wonderfully made. Wonderful are your works; my soul knows it very well. My frame was not hidden from you, when I was being made in secret, intricately woven in the depths of the earth. Your eyes saw my unformed substance; in your book were written, every one of them, the days that were formed for me, when as yet there was none of them. (PSALM 139:14-16)

Molly's life, Dennis reminds us, was a gift from God, a testimony of His glory, a song to His praise. Her life was one of great purpose. She fulfilled her destiny, her created reason for being. He then reminds us of the Bible's description of death—for those who believe in Christ—as falling asleep. So confident were first-century Christians that the dead were merely sleeping that the word *cemetery* is derived from their Greek word for a dormitory. Those who "sleep" are waiting to be awakened—awakened on the great and glorious day when the Lord comes again.

We sit and absorb the consolation of these promises, words which soothe the fresh wounds of our souls. And then a little story is told that adds another layer of comfort and perspective.

I am standing on the seashore. A ship at my side spreads her white sails to the morning breeze and starts for the blue ocean. She is an object of beauty and strength and I stand and watch her until, at length, she hangs like a speck of white cloud just where the sea and the sky come down to mingle with each other. And then I hear some-one at my side saying, "There, she's gone!"

Gone where? Gone from my sight, that is all. She is just as large in mast and hull and spar as she was when she left my side, and just as able to bear her load of living freight to the place of destination. Her diminished size is in me, not in her.

And just at the moment when someone at my side says, "There, she's gone," there are other eyes watching her coming, and there are other voices ready to take up the glad shout, "Here she comes!" And, that is dying![1]

The conclusion of our celebration is deeply moving and most holy. We feel transported, by beautiful and elegant music, to the throne room of the King. As the first notes sound, Rebecca slips off the front pew to her knees. Jacob quickly moves behind her and enfolds her in his arms. Soon every family member follows their lead, encircling these two that we love so dearly, sharing this moment of pure worship.

The symphony of Molly's life was all about Jesus—coming to Him, living for Him, and in the end flying to Him in glory. There is no greater story, no more magnificent song than His. We will join Molly one day along with the millions of others who have believed in Christ for salvation. But until then, we have been led in worship as we heard His voice sing to us through Molly's life.

Why Truth Is Our Only Hope

This is my comfort in my affliction,
that Your Word has revived me.

— PSALM 119:50

Each day of Molly's life, and in the days following her death, we have depended on the bedrock of God's unchanging word to help us stand strong. Knowing that "it is impossible for God to lie," we "have strong encouragement to hold fast to the hope set before us. We have this as a sure and steadfast anchor of the soul" (Hebrews 6:18b–19a). Just as a securely anchored ship can avoid being swept out to sea in the storm, so can we stand secure even when we are severely wounded and weak. We believe more strongly than ever that there is no sure anchor but God.

His truth, the Bible, is alive and its words have power. They are the words of Someone who is alive today. It is a book of letters sent personally from Heaven to all who will listen. This is what the Bible offers—a chance to see God's written words of love, to hear His words speak to our hearts and souls, to feel the change His word can produce within. This is the Word of Truth that spoke comfort to Jacob and Rebecca and each of us on the day of Molly's death and on the day of her burial and memorial service.

We experienced the power of God through His Word—"Your word has revived me" (Psalm 119:50 NASB)—and we were strengthened (verse 28). But in the end we knew one truth above all, "Lord, to whom shall we go? You have the words of eternal life" (John 6:68). That eternal life is the hope we have for ourselves and for being reunited with Molly.

"I do not know this grief but I know what death brings—there will be no day again that is not without some measure of sadness at what, in human presumption, has been lost. Given our own direction, I do not think any of us would ask to walk through what is the most sacred territory His creatures experience. As selfless as we might want to be, allowing our loved one—allowing that beautiful beloved firstborn—to breathe air celestial is just 'asking too much.' Still, I know Rebecca and Jake are resting in the confidence that He does all things well . . . not understanding that this could be that . . . and even so, believing."

— PEGGY CAMPBELL,
whose husband died in 2005

A Pink Cloud

Following Molly's death, I moved in a fog. It was almost like I didn't know what had happened. People would ask me, "Are you okay?" and they would look at me funny.

The truth was I was tired and sad and numb.

Jacob and I were in shock.

At home on Saturday morning, I began the task of getting ready for the day that lay ahead. There was a little bit of excitement as I got ready amid my mom, sisters, and best friend Christy. It's hard to describe, but I was looking forward to being near

Molly's body again. I wanted to look my best for our little girl. I carefully did my makeup and hair and proudly put on my light pink dress to wear in her honor. As Jacob and I drove together to her funeral, I felt anxious and nervous. We talked about the logistics of the day, where we were going, what would happen next.

We pulled up in our car, just a few yards from the tent where Molly's casket sat. I suddenly felt weak.

People stood outside the tent. All eyes were on Jacob, in his pink shirt and tie, and me as we walked forward. Molly's casket was so tiny under the big green tent—a little white box with a ruffled material around the middle and on top an arrangement from Jacob's parents of beautiful pink baby roses with a few larger ones. I felt disbelief that Molly's body lay inside.

Jacob stepped up to the table and lifted the casket with both hands, remarking on how light it felt. I wanted to pick it up and run away with Molly's tiny body inside. I longed to bring her back to life. If I could only lift her from that awful box and take her home where she belonged, this would all go away, I thought. My grief was talking.

Instead of running away, we sat on a front row of chairs under the tent. I gazed intently at Molly's box, and Jacob stared at the ground. We were spent, stunned that our newborn daughter had just died less than two days ago.

We heard only bits and pieces of hope as both of our dads read God's word in an effort to point us and our families to Jesus. Then everyone sang a song. I don't remember much else except that Jacob and I had the chance to write a love letter to our daughter on a pale pink helium-filled balloon. We wanted to express our hearts, hurt, love for Molly, and our desire to see her again. Jacob wrote first and, after passing the balloon to me, sank to the ground, weeping. He was in utter pain and agony. He no longer needed help grieving.

I wrote on the balloon and then took Jacob's hand. We walked from under the tent, our families gathered behind us. Together, Jacob and I let the pink balloon slip from our fingers into the blue sky. We stood there a long time watching the balloon soar higher and higher.

Then we walked quietly and contemplatively over to the church for the memorial service. Molly's photographs drew us down the center aisle. For a few moments, I stood in front of the pictures of Molly with her pink blanket over my shoulder. Then we sat on the front row.

During the service we had a short sharing time with a few of our siblings telling their memories of Molly and prayers for us. But we also wanted to share all about Molly with the people we loved, so Jacob and I each took a turn at the microphone. I don't remember all we said or how we were able to stand there, *other than I believe the power of God sustained us. It is a mystery to me, but it was real.*

Outside the church, after the service, all those who had come joined together in a circle around both of our families. Each person held a pink balloon with a long, curly string attached. I whispered, "I love you Molly," as Jacob and I let go of one more balloon with ninety-nine others. It was beautiful to watch the balloons float into the sky, a pink cloud from a cloud of witnesses.

I think of that moment sometimes when I go back to visit Molly's doorway. The doorway—that's what I call her grave. I got the idea from Pam, my sweet mother-in-law who gave me this poem by Calvin Miller:

> I once scorned ev'ry fearful thought of death,
>
> When it was but the end of pulse and breath,
>
> But now my eyes have seen that past the pain
>
> There is a world that's waiting to be claimed.
>
> Earthmaker, Holy, let me now depart,
>
> For living's such a temporary art.
>
> And dying is but getting dressed for God,
>
> Our graves are merely doorways cut in sod.[3]

Sometimes, when I want to talk to Molly, I go sit by her doorway and journal.

I'm not talking to the ground. I'm sitting on Heaven's doorstep.

Molly's Music Lingers

> The only right attitude towards suffering is worship,
> or humble self-surrender.
>
> — JOHN R. W. STOTT

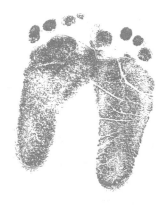

Dennis and I flew home on Tuesday morning. The long journey with Rebecca and Jacob had caught up with me, and I felt like I could sleep for twenty-four hours. When I walked in the door and did a quick scan of the house, I felt empty. Everything was like it had been when we left. But I was not like I was when I left. I missed Molly, and I didn't want to return to normal life.

I tried to take a nap and eventually dozed off for a short while, but my mind was whirling with the memories, the songs, the verses, the hundreds of evidences of God's mercy and love. When I got up, Dennis was opening the stacks of mail. I thought, *I know this has to be done, but I'm not ready for the routine.* We'd been on holy ground and experienced the power of the Almighty. We'd been touched by Molly, and I didn't want the song of her sweet life to fade into silence. The nearness of God was now more valuable to me than ever. Molly had led me there.

I imagined her dancing with Jesus, laughing in glory. I went to my bookshelf to find a book of Puritan prayers that I'd discovered a few years ago. I remembered the first prayer, "The Valley of Vision," spoke to where our family was:

> Thou hast brought me to the valley of vision,
>
> where I live in the depths but see thee in the heights; . . .
>
> Let me learn . . . that the valley is the place of vision.
>
> Lord, in the daytime stars can be seen from the deepest wells,
>
> and the deeper the wells the brighter thy stars shine;
>
> Let me find thy light in my darkness,
>
> thy life in my death, thy joy in my sorrow,
>
> thy grace in my sin, thy riches in my poverty,
>
> thy glory in my valley.[1]

I want to stay in this deep well where we've seen stars shine. I want to stay in this valley that I may continue to see the light of the glory of God's great goodness. Yes, we have been touched by Molly, but it was God who gave her and took her and revealed Himself to us in many ways that we might know Him more fully.

We have encountered the Almighty in the valley.

"God was sufficient for us in Molly's life and continues to be in the ongoing pain of her death. And He will be enough for us in whatever the future brings."

— REBECCA RAINEY MUTZ

Carrying the Pieces Forward

Right after the funeral, when we were back home, things felt especially weird, as if giving birth to Molly had never happened. There was no baby, just an empty nursery. We never brought Molly home. We'd had a whole other life for one week and then stepped back into our previous life, our "before," only I wasn't pregnant anymore and now I was producing milk, but there was no baby to nurse.

I was so very tired. Jacob and I slept a lot and didn't feel like eating. We were still in shock, I suppose. We told ourselves to go back to our everyday routines, and that this was what we had to do. I went for a long stretch where I didn't cry every day, but I thought about Molly all the time.

Jacob and I began to journal as a way to put words to what we felt. It helped us process what was so jumbled up in our hearts. My heart was heavy and yet light at the same time. I was sad, missing our sweet Molly so much, but delighted she was with Jesus, singing and dancing with no pain, no tears, no sorrow.

Our counselor acknowledged the rush of both joy and sorrow. He said: "Your emotions are going to play catch up."

In July, a month after Molly's birth and death, more deep sadness did come, and other emotions that surprised us and caught us off guard. The smallest things suddenly set us into tears. Jacob described this as our new life in waves—waves of grief that come and go, some big and tall, some small and short. We never know when the waves will come. We never have any warning.

Friends we'd met with the week after Molly died had warned us of this too. They lost their first child, a daughter, a few years ago. They told us how painful it was for them, how difficult to re-enter life. Things will get harder, they said, before they get easier.

I didn't like hearing that. I wanted to feel the waves of joy from having Molly and spending a week with her. I looked at pictures of us with Molly and thought, This isn't hard, because I didn't want to forget having her. I was so proud of our week with her. I didn't want to be depressed about our loss. I was sad Molly was gone, but I was so glad that she had gone on to a better place, far better than this earth.

But I couldn't deny the struggle the day I asked a friend, Morgan, to help pick out pictures of Molly for a new frame. She had to stop after a few minutes because the pictures were so sad to her. For me, the pictures of Jacob holding Molly after she had died became most difficult to look at . . . because I know I wasn't there. I became angry that I didn't stay as long as he did and hold her more. Why didn't I stay longer? Why did I leave? No one made me leave. I had just decided Molly was gone and I was ready to go.

I wished I hadn't.

I knew that wishing wouldn't do anything for us except make things harder, more difficult to bear, but I began to wish many things: If I'd not had the need for sleeping or eating, I would have stayed by Molly's bedside the entire time. I would have seen her more, taken more pictures, kissed more of her sweet skin, and held her little hands more. I would have been able to calm her down when the nurses changed her bedding or rolled her onto her side. I would have asked to hold her more even if it meant my back would ache.

More waves of anger hit me. I was angry at how different and empty life now felt. I was angry that other people seemed to be moving on with their lives, having healthy babies, waking up at odd hours to calm their crying babies and feed them, just being back in the swing of life as it was for them.

I told Jacob that while a lot of people still thought of us and of Molly, and prayed

fervently for us, no one had the physical reminder like we did that she was gone. No

one else had a decorated nursery with an empty crib. For us, the loss was continual,

throughout each and every day. I missed our old life, our old normal. We didn't get

to go back to the old normal anymore. Jacob told me that we now had to learn to

adjust together to our new normal. I found this hard and did not want to deal with

it. Life was forever changed—different, scary. The waves were getting bigger.

By September, three months after Molly's death, I started to see the patterns of the

waves, their rhythms, as I shared our story. Initially I'd be fine, enjoying conversa-

tion about Molly with people who cared. Sometime after or during those moments,

I found myself overwhelmed by feelings of sadness, jealousy, or anger. More often

than not, I was just sad and missed our daughter. The anger always surprised me

most, and left me feeling bad, like I shouldn't feel that way. I'm still learning that

all my emotions are okay, part of the process, and good for me to feel. It's better

than feeling numb, although there are days when I wish for the numbness to return.

Being numb can be easier.

So can distraction. As the busyness of life returns I sometimes forget to grieve or

cry. But the forgetting doesn't last. It's momentary, and as effective on grief as

trying to keep the lid on a boiling pot of water. Before long, the grief pushes up the lid and the steam and water escape and sizzle. Tears stream down my face as I watch my nephew kneeboard and I realize that we won't be able to watch Molly learn how to kneeboard or water ski. I won't be teaching her how to bake cupcakes and decorate them with all sorts of colored icings. Jacob won't be taking her out on dates and interviewing the boys that want to date her or hearing from the young man who wants to marry her. We won't walk her down the aisle to give her away because we've already given her away to Jesus.

I thought of this at a wedding we attended, where I unexpectedly met the parents of a friend of mine.

Sitting in the church waiting for the ceremony to start, my friend, Jessica, asked me how I was doing, and listened with a tender heart. I told her what I'd begun to tell everyone who asks: It's one day at a time, one foot forward, as we continue to grieve and mourn our loss of sweet Molly.

My friend said our story gave her new perspective for what her parents, seated next to her, had gone through. They, too, lost their firstborn, a son, at birth.

Jessica's dear mom, Terry Cline, later came to sit by me at the reception. She asked me through tears about our Molly. She didn't say a word about her own loss, but listened as I told her a brief version of Molly's story. I was showing her the pictures that I keep on my phone when her husband came over to look. She gave me back the phone and with tears in her eyes said, "You'll always be Molly's mommy, and Molly is beautiful."

I was so proud. I didn't cry, but instead beamed with the biggest smile, relishing the moment with this dear woman who understood my pain.

Jessica's dad, Leroy Cline, stayed behind me as his wife walked back to her chair. For several seconds I didn't realize he was still there, wiping his eyes. I heard a sniffle and turned around just as he knelt by my chair and put his arm around my shoulders. He told me he was so sorry for Jacob's and my loss.

"The hurt will never go away," he said, "but it will get easier."

His tears told me that the pain was still there for him more than twenty-eight years after his own loss. He knew the pain that I felt more than anyone else in that room.

I thanked him for his tears. I've loved seeing the tears of others, so beautiful and dear. Tears communicate so much to us. When people feel free to share their tears, we know that they are walking with us, sharing our burden.

My own tears take many forms, and can be seen in Molly's Journal:

Dear Molly,

Three months must seem like three minutes to you, but to us it has seemed like eternity. We miss you dearly. We also find it in our hearts to celebrate your being with Jesus. We dream about what it would be like to be there with you and with our King. Do you have parties every month like we imagine? Do you get cupcakes and party hats? Do you get the balloons we send you?

I sit in your room and gaze upon your precious face and all the features that make you so unique and so Molly! I still smile when I think about how long your feet are. I bet they help you run fast through the soft green grass with the light of Christ shining on your beautiful face. And your long, gorgeous fingers help you pick the beautiful flowers and feel their soft and silky petals. Your perfect eyes take in the beauty that surrounds you, beauty that we can only fathom and dream about seeing someday soon. Your lungs don't fight for oxygen anymore and neither does your heart race to keep up with the demands of your little, broken body.

We send you sweet hugs and kisses daily. We look forward with eager anticipation to the day we meet up with you in the heavenly realm!

Until the day . . .

Mommy

By October, four months to the day of Molly's death, Jacob and I were enjoying a visit from two of his brothers and his sister, Kelli. Michael and Mark had been unable to meet Molly when she was born because they were on a mission trip, so we decided to take them by Molly's doorway for a visit.

I clipped some flowers from our yard and talked to the boys about her. I loved visiting Molly's doorway because it reminded me of where she is and how she feels no pain, no fear. Also, because this was the last place I was close to her physical body, the part of her that I carried and nurtured for so long.

As I told the boys how much we miss Molly, I thought that seemed such an understatement. The more we tried to explain, the more our words felt inadequate. After a while, I realized, words seem so silly to explain the desires of my mommy heart and all the memories I have of our precious daughter. She is loved and missed more than I knew possible and that loss only grows.

In November, I encountered one of the hardest times of grief. Jacob was on a business trip, and my sweet friend, Jenny Beth, had come over for the evening. She encouraged me as I told her how sad I was.

After Jenny Beth left, I went upstairs and crawled carefully into Molly's crib. I wanted to be where she should have been. Curled up in a ball, I lay there and cried for a long time and then fell asleep.

The next morning at church, I saw my brother, Ben, who must have noticed my eyes swollen from crying. I told him I needed a hug, which he gladly gave, a great big, long, bear hug. It was so wonderful, but still I needed more. I drove to Molly's doorway and journaled, then laid down to rest and fell asleep. I was so tired from mourning.

The waves were powerful now. The grief was getting stronger. I knew we would never forget.

Jacob felt it too. He wrote about the mounting grief in a November 13 journal entry:

After Molly went to be with Jesus, Becca wanted to start trying right away to get pregnant again, even though her ob-gyn advised her to wait six months. I wanted to make sure we had time to process our grief. I didn't want to feel like we would be trying to replace Baby A with Baby B.

Well, Becca is queen and she correctly reminded me, "The Lord opens the womb and closes the womb."

When July and August came and went with no pregnancy, I began to feel really disappointed, which surprised me. But it had been two and a half long months since I held Molly against my chest and felt her warm, soft baby skin, and smelled her sweet, new-baby scent.

Then it was September, and we felt even more the disappointment of an empty cradle and an empty womb. Well-meaning people would instruct us it was time to start trying again, or ask, "Are you trying to get pregnant?" It wasn't the question or advice that bothered me so much as why they asked, like maybe they were thinking, "When are you going to get over this, replace Molly, and crank out another kid?"

In October, we were nearly certain "it" would finally happen, after all this was when we had determined getting pregnant again made sense. Plus we had now been trying longer than we had when Molly was conceived.

Again, disappointment.

The book of Proverbs reminded us that "a man plans his course, but the Lord determines his steps" (Proverbs 16:9 NIV). So we determined to open our hands, palms up, and let the Lord take it over.

This morning, at about 5:15 a.m., I kissed Becca, who, as she awoke, told me we should take a pregnancy test. She thought she was late. I immediately felt a great sense of joy. Finally, I thought, this month must be God's timing! I love my wife, so I tore back the sheets and was ready to go do the test. But Rebecca reminded me, "Let's pray first."

Right. I told myself, I knew that! I should be more of a spiritual leader! We prayed for a few minutes and thanked God for His provisions, His grace, and abounding love. We asked Him to help us to keep trusting Him. Then Becca did her thing to the pregnancy wizard stick and we nervously waited. Actually she wanted to watch the lines, but I couldn't do it. She said we had to wait three minutes so I went and did push-ups, kissed her, reread the test instructions: one line equals not pregnant, two lines equals yes. We had made it past the seemingly endless 180-second wait. It was now 5:24 a.m. We picked up the test strip, and . . . One line. Just one, pathetic, miserable line.

Not pregnant.

I couldn't believe it. There we were, trusting God for one whole month, and He didn't even hold up His end of the deal.

But that was the point: This wasn't a deal.

In his book *A Grief Observed*, C. S. Lewis writes that we can say we trust the strength of a rope to hold us until we are blue in the face, but until there actually comes a time where we decide if we are going to let that rope hold us, we really don't know if we trust it.

How dependent I need to be on Christ, how patient I need to be in His timing. As I write this, I am thankful He first loved me.

He first was patient with me.

We were about to be tested even more. Five months after Molly died, I thought about how time has gone by almost without me. I wished it would stop—stop or hurry up, one of the two. I mentioned to our grief group that I was feeling like I was still back in June, physically even. There were still warm days here in Colorado, and the sun would shine in November like on a hot June day. But my closet, full of sweaters, jeans, and warm socks, reminded me that June was gone along with Molly.

I wished I knew how to prepare for the holidays that were coming like a freight train. I wanted to skip them, actually. I didn't want to think about what I was thankful for over Thanksgiving, even though I remained so thankful for Molly. I didn't want Christmas this year, as the quiet house and empty nursery seemed to mock me. I didn't know how to bring Molly into our holidays either. Should I buy her a stocking to hang next to ours on the mantle? Should I wrap a present for her and place it under the tree?

It seemed so silly, but several times in those first five months, I almost bought Molly a little dress, some cute socks, or a sweet blanket. At a Gap outlet once, Jacob and I were searching for something when we came across the baby section. Darling outfits and dresses were paired with cute shoes and tiny hats—things I wouldn't have thought twice about buying for Molly before she died. Suddenly, I wished I could have gone shopping while she was here, to have bought something for my daughter, just for the simple fact that I was a mommy and had a daughter to dress. I watched other moms sift through racks and shelves and hold up cute dresses on their two-year-olds, or grab a few onesies for their infants. How I wanted that. I wanted the mundane, perfectly wonderful times to drag the kids to Target to try on a new pair of shoes. I want to be the mom who came by the bakery just to get a cookie for her three-year-old.

Unfortunately life doesn't let you skip the hard parts. Thanksgiving and Christmas came unbidden. The seasons continued to change around me, even though in my soul it was still June and the sun was shining and my daughter was snuggled up, warm, against my heart.

Am I sad Molly is gone? Yes.

Am I angry? Sometimes.

Am I bitter? No.

I don't want to be bitter because all I have to hold on to is the fact that God is still good even when bad things happen. This message has been hitting home more and more lately.

Our pastor talked about this in church, how God says no to some prayers, and then sometimes says wait.

God knows what is best for us, just like my parents knew when I was little and wanted to play in the street or eat chocolate for every meal. I may never see the reason behind why God took Molly so early. For now, I'm okay with that. I'm not sure I want to know why right now anyway. I am reminded: it is what it is, and I have the choice about how I respond.

Recently, I was asked, "Do you wrestle with God over Molly's life?"

"No," I answered. "I don't ask why because even if He did give me a reason I don't think it would make me feel any better. I just trust Him. I trust that He has a reason . . . That sounds so much like a church answer, but it's so true. God is in control and I'm not, and I'm so glad He is.

The truth is every day I wish it were different. But seeing the impact Molly's had on so many people has lessened the blow a little bit, just a little.

Jacob asked me, "If you could take away everything Molly's done, all the impact, to have her back, would you?"

Oh, I'd say yes. But I'm so proud of her because she did so much. I don't know what it's like to have a child longer than seven days, but I can imagine that other parents pray for and desire their children to have the kind of impact that Molly had in their lifetime. And she did that in seven days.

The journey of grief and discovery and change is not over, and from what I've learned it won't ever really be over. I'm glad because that means Molly's influence on me and others won't end either. Her life goes on, just in a different place than mine.

In February I wrote her another letter:

Little Miss Molly,

Did you ever think someone would write a book about you? Well, that someone is me. Your short little life reflects the magnitude of all that God has done, and that is certainly worth writing about. Your Mimi and I are tackling this project and it is well under way.

We have a short deadline because we want it to be in print in time for your birthday. What a birthday present that will be!

In order to help me write, I've pulled out the Kleenex and the videos that your uncles and aunts put together for us. Seeing you again in video was so good for my heart. It helped to remember and refocus my thoughts. It also helped me to grieve again. I haven't cried for you in a while and it always feels so good to cry. It heals my heart to see your eyes open and hear your little cry from those first few hours in the NICU.

To say that I miss you is such an understatement. I've been thinking lately that my words are so inadequate for how I am feeling. I long for you, Molly. To touch you and feel your heart beating or your fingers clasp mine. We love you so much and miss you even more. You have continued to touch our hearts and cause us to move closer to the heart of God. We knew our lives would be changed forever by you, but we had no idea how much or how significantly.

Until that day arrives . . .

Hugs and kisses,

Mommy

Molly has given us a deeper perspective on life. We look at God differently. My relationship with Him is much closer than it was before.

We hope and dream of a little brother or sister for Molly. Still, as we look to the future we feel some fear. Several people have asked me recently: What if what happened with Molly happens all over again?

What if . . . ?

I think about that sometimes, but Jacob and I know: If it happens again, we will go through it again. We trust God will still be there, will still have a plan, will still be holding us.

God was sufficient for us in Molly's life and continues to be in the ongoing pain of her death. And He will be enough for us in whatever the future brings.

We trust Him.

We heard His voice in Molly's life.

She changed everything.

My Prayer for You

My Prayer for You

Dear Reader,

It is my prayer that when you go through a difficult season or trial, my story may bring you comfort and peace. I would never wish our circumstances on anyone, but only desire that what sufferings and challenges God does bring into your life will serve to draw you closer to Him as it did me. We are never promised a life without pain, but rather we are promised that the God of all comfort is close to the brokenhearted. No matter how much your heart hurts, you can be assured that God hears your prayers and knows each tear that you shed. You are not alone. There are many books I've found helpful during this difficult season, and in one especially, there is a letter to a father who just lost his third son to illness. What his dear friend writes is encouraging and so true:

I do hope and pray that God may give you grace to exercise a faith which will humble, comfort and cheer your inmost soul. But if you cannot so believe, at least lay your hands on your bleeding and darkened spirit, and drag it along the way of duty. Follow the Master's will, in comfort if you can, but follow it. He will bring you out into a pleasant place in His own time.[1]

We prayed as we wrote this book that it would glorify God and meet you in your time of need or guide you to help someone else in need. May you find the hope and encouragement you need here.

Rebecca Rainey Mutz

END NOTES

DAY ONE *Friday* **A NEW KIND OF WAITING**

Epigraph. John Piper, "Governor of All," *WORLD,* October 6, 2001, 37.

1. Adapted from: Andrée Seu, "When Nothing's Happening," *WORLD,* December 24, 2005.

2. Adrian Rogers, Adrianisms: *The Wit and Wisdom of Adrian Rogers Vol. Two* (Memphis: Love Worth Finding Ministries, 2007), 144.

3. Warren W. Wiersbe, *The Bible Exposition Commentary* (Colorado Springs: David C. Cook, 2003), 221.

4. Stu Weber, *Tender Warrior: Every Man's Purpose, Every Woman's Dream, Every Child's Hope* (Sisters, OR: Multnomah, 2006), 252.

DAY TWO *Saturday* **A SEVERE TESTING**

Epigraph. Larry Crabb, *Shattered Dreams: God's Unexpected Pathway to Joy* (Colorado Springs: Waterbrook, 2001), 4.

1. Victor Hugo, *Les Misérables,* (New York: Penguin Group, 1987), 932.

DAY THREE *Sunday* **WAITING FOR HEAVEN**

Epigraph. Tony Snow, "Cancer's Unexpected Blessings," *Christianity Today,* July 2007, 32.

1. James W. Bruce III, *From Grief to Glory: Spiritual Journeys of Mourning Parents* (Wheaton, IL: Crossway Books, 2002), 45.

2. Randy Alcorn, *Heaven* (Carol Stream, IL: Tyndale House, 2004), 77.

3. Referring to the fictional character found in C. S. Lewis' *The Chronicles of Narnia* series.

4. Charles Spurgeon, *Morning and Evening* (New Kensington, PA: Whitaker, 2001), 244.

DAY FOUR *Monday* **ENJOYING THE MOMENTS**

Epigraph. Snow, 32.

1. Helen H. Lemmel, "Turn Your Eyes Upon Jesus," in *Glad Songs,* British National Sunday School Union 1922.

2. Edith Schaeffer, *What Is a Family?* (Grand Rapids: Baker Books, 1975).

DAY FIVE *Tuesday* LEANING INTO PEACE

Epigraph. Horatio Spafford, "When Peace Like a River," 1873.

1. John Piper, *What's the Difference?* (Wheaton, IL: Crossway Books, 1990), 13.

2. Adapted from: Piper, 38.

INTERLUDE THE MASTER COMES

1. Charles Spurgeon, *Spurgeon's Sermons,* vol. 5 (Grand Rapids: Baker Books, 1985), 384-385.

DAY SIX *Wednesday* TREASURES IN THE DARKNESS

Epigraph. Spurgeon, *Morning and Evening,* 448.

1. Dr. Paul Brand and Philip Yancey, *In His Image* (Grand Rapids: Zondervan, 1997), 21-22.

DAY SEVEN *Thursday* CORONATION DAY

Epigraph. As quoted in: Glenn R. Kreider, "The God Delusion: A Theological Response," review of *The God Delusion* by Richard Dawkins, *Kindred Spirit Magazine,* summer 2008.

1. Andrée Seu, "What Is the Victory?" *WORLD Magazine,* June 7, 2003, 43.

POSTLUDE WORSHIP AND ANGUISH

Epigraph. J. I. Packer, *Great Joy: A 31-Day Devotional* (Ann Arbor: Vine Books, Servant Publications, 1998), 71.

1. Source unknown.

2. Calvin Miller, *The Divine Symphony* (Minneapolis: Bethany, 2000), 139.

MOLLY'S MUSIC LINGERS

Epigraph. John R. W. Stott, *Why Do the Innocent Suffer?* (London: Crusade Booklets, 1956), 10.

1. "The Valley of Vision," in *The Valley of Vision: A Collection of Puritan Prayers and Devotions,* ed. Arthur Bennett (Edinburg: Banner of Truth Trust, 1975), xxiv.

MY PRAYER FOR YOU

1. Bruce, 76.

AUTHORS' NOTES

COMFORTING, HELPFUL READING

Sittser, Gerald L. *A Grace Disguised: How the Soul Grows Through Loss.* Grand Rapids, MI: Zondervan, 1996. Sittser, Jerry. Expanded edition, Grand Rapids: Zondervan, 2005.

Bruce III, James W. *From Grief to Glory: Spiritual Journeys of Mourning Parents.* Wheaton, IL: Crossway Books, 2002.

Cowman, L. B.; Mrs. Charles E. Cowman; and James Reimann, ed. *Streams in the Desert.* Cowman Publications, Inc., 1925, 1953, 1965. Grand Rapids, MI: Zondervan, 1996.

Alcorn, Randy. *Heaven.* Wheaton, IL: Tyndale House, 2004.

Taylor, Rick. *When Life Is Changed Forever by the Death of Someone Near.* Eugene, OR: Harvest House Publishers, 1993.

DAILY E-MAILS TO HELP THROUGH GRIEF

Griefshare.org — This organization also produces a video-based support group curriculum.

A MEMORY KEEPING RESOURCE

Now I Lay Me Down To Sleep is a not-for-profit 501(c)(3) organization of photographers who volunteer their time and services to families experiencing the death of an infant. Contact:

Now I Lay Me Down to Sleep
7201 S. Broadway Suite #150
Littleton, CO 80122
Phone: (877) 834-5667, from 9 a.m. to 5 p.m., Mountain Standard Time
Fax: (720) 283-8998
Web site: nowilaymedowntosleep.org
E-mail: headquarters@nilmdts.org

READER'S DISCUSSION GUIDE AND BIBLE STUDY

Go to FamilyLife.com/guides for a downloadable reader's discussion guide on finding and keeping faith through loss and grief.

BARBARA RAINEY is the mother of six adult children, including Rebecca, who is her "prayed for" fourth child. She is also the "Mimi" of fourteen grandchildren. Barbara and her husband, Dennis, give leadership to FamilyLife, a ministry committed to helping marriages and families survive and thrive in our generation. She has written several books, including, *Thanksgiving: A Time to Remember, Barbara and Susan's Guide to the Empty Nest,* and *When Christmas Came.* The Raineys live in Little Rock, Arkansas. You can read more from Barbara at FamilyLifeMomblog.com.

REBECCA RAINEY MUTZ is the mother of Molly Ann and lives with her husband, Jacob, in Colorado. She enjoys the beauty of the mountains as well as exercising her desires and passions in cooking and baking. Rebecca and Jacob hope to use Molly's life as a way to share Christ with others and bring glory to God. You can read more from Rebecca on her blog: RebeccaCooks.blogspot.com.

ACKNOWLEDGMENTS

We thank God for the blessing of little Miss Molly Ann. Without her incredible entrance into our lives, we would not be who we are today. Thank you, Jesus, for the life-giving price you paid so that we might spend eternity with You and our Molly girl. And thank you, Lord, for letting us hear the music of your love song as we suffered so deeply. What an amazing gift!

To both of our families, the Mutzes and Raineys, we offer a profound thank you for your love, support, and encouragement during the week Molly was alive and in the months that have followed. Your physical presence with Rebecca and Jacob at Children's meant everything. And your practical help planning the funeral arrangements, coordinating the travel and housing of all who came, and the orchestration of the services that honored Molly's life and Jesus' sacrifice was a service of inestimable value.

To our friends who planned and served Molly's memorial dinner, cleaned our house, brought us meals, cried with us, and have supported Rebecca and Jacob so much since Molly went to be with Jesus, we are forever grateful.

To the incredible nurses and staff at The Children's Hospital in Denver, including Beth, Michelle, Diane, Lisa, Jeni, Precious, Dr. Grover, Dr. Wilkinson and many others: Thank you for giving us your best and for truly caring for us in our time of crisis.

To our editor, Jeanette Thomason, and the staff at FamilyLife Publishing for making this book possible, especially Tim Grissom and Rebecca Price. Thank you for the hours of editing, conference calls, and reading the manuscript over and over with us that it might be excellent.

And finally we offer thanks to the thousands of people worldwide who prayed for us that week and afterward, we are grateful and cannot wait to meet you all in Heaven. There we will all celebrate with great joy the victory of our King over the enemy of death. And what a party it will be!